Praise for Dan Smith's other atlases:

'Successfully educates the reader about the Middle East region and the conflicts, both historical and modern, that have led to the current situation in this part of the world.'
Library Journal

'This book shows why there is still a need for reference books, at a time when we have almost limitless access to the internet.... It decisively outscores both Google and Wikipedia on their two weakest points – context and provenance.'
International Socialist Group

'A unique atlas that will serve as a ready reference book in both high school and college settings, as well as in private homes and libraries. The book is concise yet detailed, and the information contained within its pages is easy to comprehend and is essential knowledge for anyone wanting to better understand the politics and history of this volatile region.'
History in Review

'Ever since the pre-war days of Lancelot Horabin, maps have been a time-honoured way of conveying information to activists and this series has garnered plaudits for its graphical representation of everything from climate change to the status of women. Dan Smith has already produced two for them, *The Atlas of War and Peace* and *The State of the World Atlas*, both widely and deservedly praised. This latest one is in the same, brilliantly researched and effectively presented tradition. Since the world's warmongers seem to have seized upon the Middle East as their hegemonic area of choice, this atlas ought to be in every peace worker's armoury of information.'
Morning Star

'As a source of instantly accessible information it is hard to imagine [this book] being bettered. It should be a basic reference for anyone trying to understand the complexities of the Middle East today.'
World Disarm

'Everyone should be provided with a copy of this book.'
World Affairs Report

"Invaluable...I would not be without
the complete set on my own shelves."
Times Educational Supplement

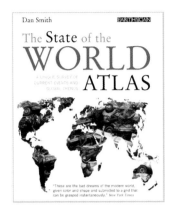

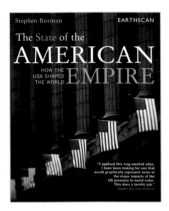

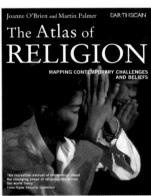

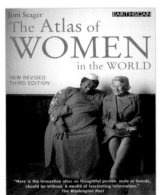

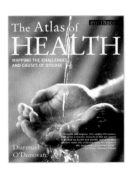

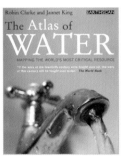

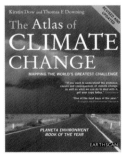

"No-one wishing to keep a grip on the reality of the world should be without
these books." *International Herald Tribune*

"Fascinating and invaluable." *The Independent*

"A new kind of visual journalism" *New Scientist*

Dan Smith is Secretary General of the London-based
international peacebuilding organization International Alert and
former Director of the International Peace Research Institute, Oslo (PRIO).
In 2002 he was awarded an OBE. He is the author of successive editions of the
The State of the World Atlas and *The Atlas of War and Peace*.

THE STATE OF THE
MIDDLE EAST

AN ATLAS OF CONFLICT AND RESOLUTION

Updated Second Edition

DAN SMITH

University of California Press, one of the most distinguished university presses in the United States, enriches lives around the world by advancing scholarship in the humanities, social sciences, and natural sciences. Its activities are supported by the UC Press Foundation and by philanthropic contributions from individuals and institutions. For more information, visit www.ucpress.edu.

University of California Press
Berkeley and Los Angeles, California

ISBN: 978-0-520-25753-5 (pbk. : alk. paper)

The Library of Congress has cataloged an earlier version of this book as follows:

Library of Congress Cataloging-in-Publication Data

Smith, Dan, 1951–.
The state of the middle east : an atlas of conflict and resolution / Dan Smith.
p.   cm.
Includes bibliographical references and index.
ISBN 978-0-520-24867-0 (cloth : alk. paper)
ISBN 978-0-520-24868-7 (pbk. : alk. paper)
1. Middle East—Maps.   2. Africa, North—Maps.   3. Middle East—History.
4. Africa, North—History.   5. Middle East—Foreign relations—North Africa.
6. Africa, North—Foreign relations—Middle East.   7. Middle East—Economic
conditions.   8. Africa, North—Economic conditions.   I. Title.

G2205.S6   2006
327.56061—dc22   2007630183

Produced for the University of California Press by
Myriad Editions Limited
Brighton, UK
www.MyriadEditions.com

Edited and co-ordinated for Myriad Editions by
Candida Lacey, Martine McDonagh and Elizabeth Wyse
Design and graphics by
Isabelle Lewis and Corinne Pearlman
Maps created by Isabelle Lewis

Printed on paper produced from sustainable sources.
Printed and bound in Hong Kong through Lion Production
under the supervision of Bob Cassels, The Hanway Press, London.

15   14   13   12   11   10   09   08
10   9   8   7   6   5   4   3   2   1

CONTENTS

The Middle East is not the only conflict-torn and complex region of the world. In fact, if measured by war deaths compared to column inches and newscast minutes in the world news media, the Middle East receives disproportionate attention compared to either South Asia or Central Africa. But there is something different about the Middle East. That 'something different' has much to do with religion, also with oil, with its geographic location, and with its history. From these factors has grown the region's strategic significance, which in turn explains the political attention the region receives from the world's great powers, and from that comes the news media coverage. And that, of course, is far from the only kind of attention that the region gets. For all of this mass of information, however, most people outside the Middle East understand it in a remarkably selective way. The emphasis of general awareness and interest falls heavily on Israel/Palestine, joined by Iraq in the past six or seven years and even more recently by Iran. Intermittently, other countries and issues get a look in – when oil prices rise, when there is a major political issue at stake. It is the ambition of this atlas to give an averagely informed reader a regional overview, a chance to see both the diversity and unity of the region in a single, digestible work.

Inevitably, this has necessitated a different kind of selectivity – not selecting between countries, but making choices about how far into their history and politics to go. As a result, this book by no means replaces any of the many excellent works looking in fine-grained detail at issues and events in individual countries. Like other works that attempt to look more broadly at the region, I hope this book offers something else – a sense of the way in which events and issues interlock with each other across the region, and a sense of some of the long-term trends at work in shaping the region and defining its future.

Events in the region keep unfolding. In the months just before the first edition was published in 2006, for example, after it was too late to insert anything new into the atlas, came the war in Lebanon. Similarly, as this edition is prepared for press, the UN Security Council has just agreed a new set of sanctions against Iran because of its nuclear enrichment, and Israel has launched military action against Gaza in retaliation for Hamas militants in Gaza launching Qassem rockets at Israel.

There is no sign in the current trend of events that the region will find a new stability in the very short term, notwithstanding a succession of high level initiatives and the efforts of high powered UN envoys. And in longer perspective, it is striking how many of the most significant problems of today grew directly from problems that were already identifiable as the region moved out of the European colonial era. It is, perhaps, by addressing those underlying problems that the possible foundations of future peace could be laid.

Dan Smith
London, 2008

What happens in the Middle East affects people all over the planet in a way that is not true of all regions of the world. Because of oil, what transpires there can have profound economic impact and its conflicts have a way of involving other parts of the world, both because of the intervention of outside powers and because of the export of violence to other areas. As a result, the region is rarely out of the international news headlines and is the focus of numerous expert studies and official reports. And since the Middle East has a long history of civilization and has long been a region of special global significance, it is the focus of a plethora of scholarly books as well as headlines in the news media.

The roots of the Middle East's global significance, however, go deeper than oil, strategy and political conflict. This is the region where three world religions began. Jerusalem is part of what has been called the sacred geography of Judaism, Christianity and Islam alike. It is therefore a region where for many people – both those who live there and those who do not – spirituality and politics come together. The region's political issues are often discussed with a quite evangelical fervour by people far away. It is a region whose issues get under the skin of rational political discussion, even among the religiously sceptical.

CONFLICT AND RESOLUTION

This book explores issues in conflict. It looks at where violent conflicts have been brought to an end, assessing how stable the resulting peace is. It looks at the continuing violent conflicts, and identifies what would be necessary for them to come to an end. And it looks over the region as a whole to give an idea of the possible basis for greater peace and more equitably shared prosperity.

The intention of this book is to open a door for people who are not experts on the Middle East, but who are interested and concerned by the region's conflicts and its prospects for peace. Facts without context – especially today's facts without the context of history – do not really aid the process of understanding issues as complex and deep as those in this region. The atlas is about the contextual outlines within which events day to day can be more readily understood. Because it takes a general look across the Middle East's horizon, those who are expert on any of the countries or issues of the region will not find much if anything that is new to them, except insofar as highly specialized expertise often makes a comparative view difficult.

KNOWLEDGE AND CONTROVERSY

Understanding the region is not easy for most people outside it and the welter of information and analysis does not actually help. An enormous part of the daily reality of most people in the Middle East is – just the same as elsewhere – of little interest to international news managers. So what we find when we look at what is available for most people to read or watch is a very detailed but strangely two-dimensional picture – full of facts, without much context – when we actually want and need something simpler yet three-dimensional.

A further problem is that conflict breeds controversy, and conflicts in the Middle East breed particularly fervent controversies. The heated disputes generated by issues in the Middle East affect not only political leaders but also reporters, commentators, experts and scholars. Observing bitter arguments between deeply held but incompatible views, it often seems there is no room for some of the commonplaces of everyday conversation. Instead of acknowledging that there can be genuine misunderstandings or confusion and uncertainty about facts, accusations of bad faith abound as the partisans of different positions choose their facts and effectively deny space for an independent point of view. The implication often seems to be that not already holding the right view is inexcusable. This is inescapably alienating for anybody who has doubts about what is happening, about its causes, about the balance of rights and wrongs, and about what can or should be done.

Beyond that, there are meta-controversies about how the region should be studied. For example, a considerable body of traditional American and European scholarship about the region is derided by other scholars – both from the region and from outside it – as Orientalism. Despite the extensive research it has entailed, this body of scholarship is accused of constructing a mythical version of the region, often emphasizing what it depicts as the magic and mystery of the region, instead of describing and explaining its reality. The position of this way of thinking is not currently strong among academic specialists, yet it remains influential in public perceptions of the region. Its critics see it as essentially, though not always consciously, a product of the desire of the leading western powers to control the Middle East.

DEFINING THE MIDDLE EAST

Controversy and confusion about the Middle East start with its name – Middle of what and East of where? It was initially a British term, now widely translated and used. It is not only audibly European but also identifiably imperial in origin; the region was in the middle of a swathe of the world from Morocco to the Philippines that European powers fought to bring under their sway.

There is significant uncertainty, and contention too, about what is included in the region. In British usage in the early 20th century, it referred to Arabia, Mesopotamia, the Gulf and Persia. The term 'Near East' was used to refer to the Balkans, Anatolia, the Levant and Egypt, while the 'Far East' covered Southeast Asia, China, Korea and Japan. In some contemporary usage, the term 'Middle East' goes as far west as Morocco, includes Sudan in the south, and reaches to Pakistan and Afghanistan in the east. The National Geographic Atlas of the Middle East leaves out Pakistan, Afghanistan and Sudan along with most of North Africa, but includes Cyprus and Turkey. The reason for this lack of a universally agreed definition of the region is that the very concept of the Middle East is political. In defining it, judgements are made about some of the key issues that preoccupy it and the key factors that constitute it.

The region has been shaped by the interplay of six key historical, cultural and contemporary factors – Islam, the Ottoman Empire, European colonialism, the foundation of the state of Israel, oil and the role of the USA. The result of these factors is to tie a region together in a series of closely related economic, political, strategic and social challenges.

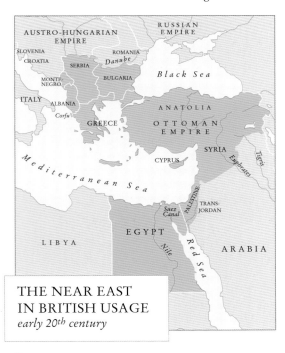

THE NEAR EAST
IN BRITISH USAGE
early 20th century

8

On this basis it would be wrong to leave out the North African states to Egypt's west. It would likewise be wrong to exclude Iran, which is intricately and inextricably part of the region's political, social and cultural development, and which faces development dilemmas that are distinctively similar to those of the rest of the region.

On the other hand, it would be misleading to include Sudan. Though it is a country where Islam is strong and where there is oil, the development dilemmas Sudan has faced over the past 50 years of independence and continues to face today are distinctively different compared to those of the Middle East. They bear far more resemblance to those of sub-Saharan Africa and spring from some of the same historical sources. Similarly, it would be inappropriate to bring in Pakistan or Afghanistan. They are both Islamic countries, but their recent histories and current dilemmas are shaped by forces and problems that are in key respects distinct from those of the Middle East.

This much will be generally agreed by most readers, if only because many books make the same judgements. American readers may be less used than European readers to the idea of the Maghreb being in the Middle East, but they will probably have come across treatments of North Africa and the Middle East as a single region, so it is not a particularly unfamiliar concept.

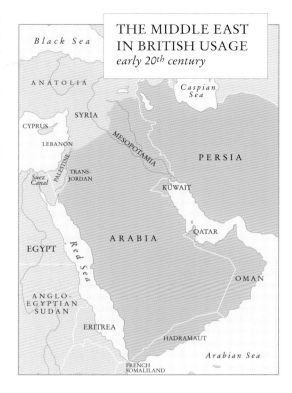

THE MIDDLE EAST
IN BRITISH USAGE
early 20th century

Equally straightforward is a decision not to include Cyprus in an atlas on the Middle East. Though the National Geographic Atlas is not alone in including Cyprus in the region, that can only be on the basis of the geographic proximity; the island's strong Hellenic links and the European orientation evident among Turkish Cypriots and Greek Cypriots alike make it more relevant to the current reality in Cyprus to see it as part of Europe. More contentious, perhaps, is the decision not to include Turkey.

TURKEY

The academic field of Middle East studies usually includes Turkey. There are people – experts on their subject – who will look at this atlas and feel that by not focusing on Turkey it misses an important aspect of the region. It is, however, a deliberate decision not to treat Turkey as part of the region. Turkey is included in the book when its present or past touches closely the affairs of the region, in much the same way as Britain, France and the USA are also included.

This judgement would neither receive universal support nor universal disapproval. A quick look is enough to reveal the diversity of definitions of the region. For example, to take one academic programme, the University of Texas Centre for Middle Eastern Studies lists Turkey as part of the Middle East. So do PBS and the CIA *World Factbook*, while the *Columbia Electronic Encyclopaedia* includes only 'the Asian part of Turkey'. On the other hand, the US State Department places Turkey in 'Europe and Eurasia', the Council on Foreign Relations puts it in 'Europe/Russia', and the BBC includes it in Europe. What is the reason for this range of opinion on the issue?

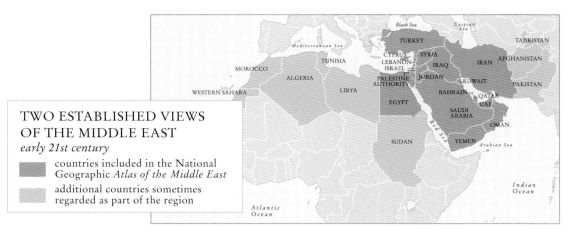

To European and North American eyes and ears, there is much that is Middle Eastern about Turkey, and the capital of the Ottoman Empire – that was so important in shaping the Middle East – was Istanbul, where the mosques and the minarets are immediately striking to the most casual glance across the cityscape. However, Turkey looks at its most Middle Eastern if the comparison is made with the Western Europe of London, Paris, Berlin, Amsterdam, Rome and Madrid. To anybody who is familiar with Southeastern Europe, there is much in modern Turkey that looks, sounds and feels strikingly familiar. That is hardly surprising, since the history of the Balkans is yoked as securely to Turkey's by the Ottoman Empire as is the history of the Middle East.

The result of the long period of Ottoman domination, however violently and completely it has been rejected by Bulgaria, Greece and the countries of the Western Balkans, is immediately evident to a visitor to the region. It can be tasted in the cuisine, seen in some of the architecture, heard in the music and, more subtly, experienced in many aspects of custom and attitude.

But it is in the issues of power, politics and conflict that the strongest reason lies for not seeing Turkey as part of the Middle East. As historical context, it is worth noting that it was not Turkey that produced the Ottoman Empire, but the collapse of the Empire that produced Turkey. Though the Ottomans had long been referred to as Turks, the country of that name was not formed until after the Ottoman Empire had perished. Mustafa Kemal Atatürk, the brilliant general and charismatic leader who led Turkey to independence and

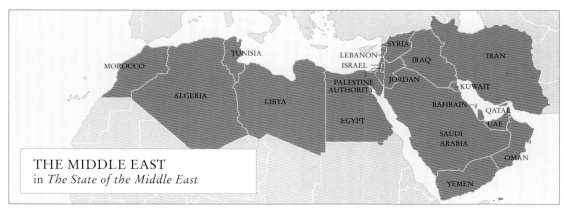

THE MIDDLE EAST
in *The State of the Middle East*

dominated its politics for a further decade and a half until his death, turned the new country towards Europe. He enforced modernity and secularism, opting to make the new state strong by learning hard lessons from the strongest states on the international stage. The process was painful, often brutal, and was deeply contested. It is, moreover, not complete today. Yet because of the course he set, Turkey was never colonized by the Europeans, was no more affected by the foundation of Israel than its neighbour Greece, has been a member of NATO for over 50 years, and is today a candidate for membership of the European Union.

Despite its own formal and political commitment to negotiate Turkey's candidacy, the EU remains visibly uncertain as to whether it really wants Turkey as a member state. Partly that is because it is suffering from expansion fatigue, partly because of racism against Turks and religious prejudice against Muslims, and partly because of uncertainty about whether Turkey is really part of Europe. The definition of what constitutes Europe is perhaps not quite as uncertain and arguable as with the Middle East, but there are question marks over the regional attribution of Turkey and some other countries. Not least, the question of whether Russia is European has long been debated back and forth.

There is no need and no intention to get distracted into an effort to resolve the issue of Europe's borders here. But it is worth noting in passing that the Middle East is not the only region whose extent is hard to fix and that Turkey is not the only major country whose regional identity is open to discussion.

The argument that Turkey is not part of the Middle East is not the same as saying that it is part of Europe. Turkey is best regarded as a meeting point of Europe and the Middle East, not fully a part of either. The recognizably European facets of Turkey are paralleled by recognizably Middle Eastern facets. Its politics are inevitably influenced by developments in the Middle East – as are those of many countries in the world to some degree – but they are also responsive to and part of the politics of Europe. For the purposes of this atlas, it would blur what is distinctive both about Turkey and about the Middle East to treat the former as part of the latter. In the end, the definition of the Middle East's geographical extent is arbitrary and varied enough that it is an author's freedom to make a reasoned choice.

ORGANIZATION OF THE BOOK

The book begins with a section looking at what has shaped the modern Middle East. Part Two moves on to explore the contemporary conflicts within the region, their background, evolution and prospects; its organizing principle is partly thematic, so it juxtaposes conflicts that are related to each other by geographic proximity and by the issues in the conflicts, and partly chronological. Part Three is a reference section, offering a statistical overview of how the countries compare with each other in political, economic and social dimensions, and how they compare with the rest of the world.

This is an atlas of today. It draws on history to explain how the region arrived at where it now stands. This means that Part One focuses on issues of power – the Ottoman and European Empires, the role of the USA, the significance of oil and the founding of the state of Israel. This perspective takes Islam as a given, long since the majority religion of the region by the time that the historical events in Part One start to unfold. On the diversity of faith – as well as diversity in other respects such as language and ethnicity – the key information is in Part Three.

The atlas uses a variety of techniques for presenting information and analysis – text, maps, other graphics and chronologies – which are intended to be read alongside each other. Each technique is able to communicate something the others cannot, such as balancing a bare-bones presentation of the chronology of events with a discussion of the context, origins and consequences of a conflict, or providing a broader framework for an easily understandable comparison. In Part Three, for example, information in each map is placed in a world context by graphic comparison with the situation of selected other countries. Because Turkey is a meeting point between the region and Europe, that country is particularly featured in these global comparisons.

ACKNOWLEDGEMENTS
A book such as this takes considerable time and quite a team to put together. This work started in Norway at the International Peace Research Institute, Oslo, as part of its strategic programme on the Middle East entitled The Missing Peace, supported by a grant from the Norwegian Research Council, through which in 2005 the Institute was able to fund Trude Strand to work as my research assistant. She was extremely adept at finding and organizing data, lining up the contrary views and interpretations of the facts, and helping me find a way through the labyrinths of uncertainty and controversy. I am grateful to the Institute's Director, Stein Tønnesson, and the then Deputy Director and programme leader, Hilde Henriksen Waage, for their support for the project.

In the early phase of work, Ane Bræin helped define the approach and the coverage of the atlas and in the final months of the project Jennifer Martin-Kohlmorgen was an excellent research assistant. At key points, I benefited from the generosity of Stephanie Koury in alerting me to sources of information and from her knowledge about the region. I have also had the benefit of helpful comments on the almost-final text and maps from Professor Nancy Gallagher at the University of California, Santa Barbara and Dr Charles Tripp at the School of Oriental and Political Studies (SOAS) in London. And I have appreciated the supportive interest of publishers on both sides of the Atlantic, Naomi Schneider at University of California Press and Jonathan Sinclair-Wilson at Earthscan.

In thanking these colleagues, friends and institutions unreservedly, I must emphasize that while they have contributed to the book's merits they bear no responsibility for any errors of fact or interpretation.

The editorial and design team at Myriad Editions has worked on this book with flexibility, imagination and incisiveness. Martine McDonagh was the ideal editor – tough on language but nice to the author – while the cartographic design work of Isabelle Lewis and the design coordination of Corinne Pearlman continue to meet the highest standards both of inventiveness and clarity. Candida Lacey coordinated the project with the empathy and style that, after several books together, I have come to expect. I thank them all for professionalism and the pleasure of working together.

Dan Smith
London, June 2006

al-Aqsa Brigades Palestinian militant group. An off-shoot of Fatah, the largest group within the Palestine Liberation Organization.

al-Jama'a al-Islamiyya Militant Islamic group that emerged from Egyptian jails in the 1970s and responsible for most of the attacks on tourists in Egypt. Its main goal is the creation of an Egyptian Islamic state.

al-Qaida Militant Islamic organization and network responsible for the September 2001 attacks on the United States. Led by Osama bin Laden, it is classified by the US, EU and UN as a terrorist group.

Alawi Secretive religious group with pre-Islamic origins, which appears to have drawn on Islamic fundamentals.

Amal Shi'a Muslim militia formed in Lebanon in 1975. Its fight against Palestinian refugees and Hizbollah led to Syria's re-intervention in Lebanon in 1987.

Druze Islamic sect with origins in Shi'a Islam and its Ismaeli split-off, but also influenced by Greek philosophy and Christianity.

Fatwa A ruling on Islamic law given by a recognized Islamic scholar.

Free Officers Movement founded by Nasser committed to the end of British rule in Egypt. Its success prompted some Arab politicians to form similar groups to unseat contemporary governments.

Hajj Pilgrimage to Mecca held annually and a central duty of Islam.

Hamas Palestinian Islamic political organization with origins in the Muslim Brotherhood, winner of the 2006 Palestine legislative elections. Listed by the US and EU as a terrorist organization.

Hashemites Arab dynasty, hereditary sharifs (guardians) of Mecca for a millennium until 1925; their descendants now rule the Kingdom of Jordan.

Hizbollah Shi'a group formed in 1982 and based in Lebanon with both a civilian and a military branch. The US has labelled Hizbollah a terrorist organization.

Islamic Jihad Militant Islamist group based in Syria which rejects any accommodation with Israel. Labelled a terrorist organization by the US and EU.

Ismaeli Mystical Shi'a group that split from mainstream Shi'ism in the 8th century AD.

Intifada Spontaneous Palestinian uprising. First *intifada*: 1987–93; second *intifada*: 2000 onwards.

Likud Conservative party of Israel.

Majlis Arab term for legislative assembly, also used by countries with strong Islamic ties.

Maronites Members of the Eastern Catholic Church and largest Christian group in Lebanon.

Muslim Brotherhood Outlawed Islamist organization founded in Egypt in 1928.

Palestine Authority Political unit with limited authority over the administration of Gaza and parts of the West Bank. It grew out of the 1993 Oslo Accords and was established in 1994.

Popular Front for the Liberation of Palestine Nationalist organization with Marxist-Leninist ideology. One of the constituent groups forming the PLO.

Sunni Islam Main Islamic school. Sunni Muslims believe the first three successors (caliphs) to Mohammed, while not directly related, were rightly chosen from the community for their leadership abilities.

Shi'ism Second largest Islamic denomination. Shi'a Muslims do not recognize the legitimacy of the initial three Sunni caliphs. They regard members of Mohammed's family as the Prophet's natural successors.

Sykes-Picot Secret agreement between France and Britain, signed 1916, which divided the Middle East into British and French zones of influence.

Wafd Literally, 'the delegation'. Nationalist Party of Egypt, disbanded after the revolution of 1952 but reconstituted in 1978 as an opposition party. It takes its name from a delegation that was to have visited Britain in 1918 to argue for Egyptian independence.

Wahhabism Puritanical Sunni Islamic movement, dominant in Saudi Arabia and Qatar.

TRANSLITERATION AND USAGE

There are at least 12 different systems for transliterating from Arabic to Latin script. They differ in, for example, their choice of vowels or their use of 'g', 'gh', 'k', 'kh', and 'q' for the same Arabic letter and sound. Though each system has its devotees, there is ultimately no correct way to spell Arabic words in Latin script. To illustrate the result, the BBC web-site lists 21 different ways of spelling the second name of the Libyan president, not including the version used in this book – Qadhafi. In general, including in this book, system is put aside when it comes to the name of a person, movement, institution or place that is particularly well known internationally and for which one form predominates in common usage.

There is similar variation of usage when it comes to the word 'Shi'a' and its derivatives. In this book, we use Shi'a as the adjective and Shi'ite as the noun.

PART ONE · THE SHAPING OF THE MIDDLE EAST

The Middle East contains some of the first places where people gathered together in towns, some four to five thousand years ago. It is also the birthplace of three great world religions — Judaism, Christianity and Islam. At different times it has been both the source and the possession of great empires. In every part of it, the past is important, both in the form of lived traditions that shape everyday life, and in the histories of power and conflict that have swept across it and left their marks. The rights and wrongs of some of today's conflicts — not least Israel and Palestine — are routinely discussed in terms that reach back long into the past, even two thousand years back. To understand the Middle East today, it is important to understand how it was made.

In the fabric of the region's history it is possible to discern a number of patterns, factors that have shaped the region and continue to do so today. The first is Islam. Adherence to the faith broadly unites the region and distinguishes it from neighbouring regions, yet internally also marks out lines of division, not only between Muslim and Jew, for example, but between Sunni and Shi'ite. Historically, the spread of Islam and the spread of Arabic from the Arabian peninsula to the borders of modern Turkey and through North Africa were a single process. Arabic, the language of the Quran, is the language of most Middle Easterners.

Great empires have left their marks on the region. The ones whose legacies live on today are the Ottoman Empire from the 14th century CE until World War I, and the 19th- and 20th- century European empires of Britain and France. The political culture of the region owes much to the Ottomans while its political structure was effectively defined by the Europeans.

As decolonization unfolded in the mid-20th century, three further factors emerged: the state of Israel was founded in 1948; in the 1950s the USA began to move in to replace the fading French and British powers; and in the same decade, the exploitation of oil gathered pace and started to generate enormous wealth. No attempt to understand conflict and the prospects for peace or disaster in the Middle East can be complete without understanding the impact of Israel, the USA and oil.

Dome of the Rock/
Temple Mount/
Haram al-Sharif, The
Old City, Jerusalem

15

THE OTTOMAN EMPIRE

Osman, the founder of the Ottoman Dynasty and Empire in the early 1300s, was the ruler of a principality in western Anatolia on the borders of the fading Byzantine empire. He was leader of one of the groups of *Ghazis* – holy warriors for Islam – whose ethnic origins lay in central Asia. The early mission of the Ottomans was to extend the Abode of Islam.

Compared to European armies of the time, Ottoman forces were professional and efficient. There was consistent expansion in the Balkans and Anatolia throughout the 14th century, until the Ottoman Sultan unwisely challenged the invincible central Asian armies of Timur the Lame in 1402 and was crushingly defeated. The Ottoman state tottered and there was a decade of internal warfare.

Ottoman leadership, however, showed resilience as well as efficiency; central authority was steadily reasserted and expansion renewed. After a further 40 years of preparation, the Ottomans took Constantinople, completing the destruction of Byzantium. The city, renamed Istanbul, became the new Ottoman capital.

The Empire's golden age was the reign from 1520 to 1566 of the 10th Sultan, Suleiman – known in the Empire as 'the Lawgiver' and in Europe as 'the Magnificent'. His 46 years of rule involved constant military campaigning, and though his ambitions were ultimately baulked in Europe, his forces were never defeated in open battle. He extended Ottoman territories as far north as Budapest, and expanded the Empire in the Middle East.

In its prime, the Ottoman Empire controlled almost as much territory in Europe as in Anatolia and the Arab lands. Both its armed forces and the quality of its administration began to deteriorate soon after Suleiman's death, but the Empire remained formidable.

In terms of territory, the Empire was at its peak when it suffered its first important defeat since Timur. Ottoman forces were repelled by a better trained and more motivated Habsburg army in 1683 outside Vienna, followed by a further defeat in 1687 at the battle of Mohács, which freed Hungary from Ottoman control.

The next 230 years of its history was a tale of decline, but the Empire was a major factor in European and Mediterranean politics throughout the 18th century. From the early 19th century, in both North Africa and the Balkans, the Ottomans lost further territory. They lost out to European nationalists in Greece, Serbia, Croatia and ultimately Bulgaria and to breakaway rulers in North Africa, who were themselves displaced, bullied or corrupted by European power as the 19th century wore on. Where the Ottoman Empire in its glory had threatened Europe with conquest, now the European powers risked war picking over the pieces.

The Sultan was in principle the absolute ruler, but the reality depended on his capacities and his will. Increasingly, the Sultan merely reigned rather than actually ruling, and the centre of Ottoman power was weakened by competing factions. Attempts at reform in the 19th century failed repeatedly, because to be successful, reform had to overturn the existing order. The reformers themselves were members of the Ottoman elite and not fully committed to that upheaval. By the time of the Empire's final demise – its fate sealed first by the Balkan War in 1912 and then by World War I – the Sultan had no executive power. The Sultanate was finally abolished in 1922 as modern Turkey was formed under the leadership of Mustafa Kemal Atatürk.

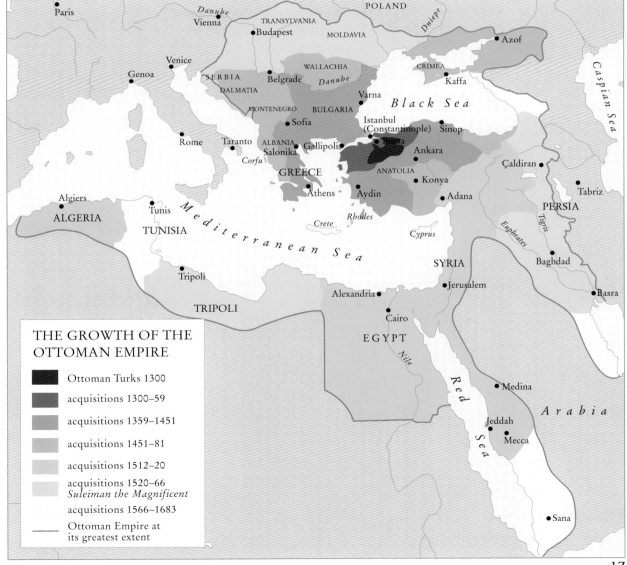

THE GROWTH OF THE OTTOMAN EMPIRE

- Ottoman Turks 1300
- acquisitions 1300–59
- acquisitions 1359–1451
- acquisitions 1451–81
- acquisitions 1512–20
- acquisitions 1520–66 *Suleiman the Magnificent*
- acquisitions 1566–1683
- Ottoman Empire at its greatest extent

The decline of the Ottoman Empire was marked by moments of extraordinary cruelty and brutality – the massacre and depopulation of the island of Chios in 1822, massacres by Turkish irregulars in the Bulgarian uprising in 1876, massacres of Armenians in Istanbul and other cities in 1895 and 1896, and of 600,000 to one million Armenians in 1915. One of the reasons for this cruelty was that Ottoman power was arbitrary. Even when the absolute power of the Sultan was more rhetoric than reality, the power of his representatives and army commanders was complete and they brooked no opposition. As opposition to Ottoman power grew both within and outside the Empire, the reaction both at the centre and in other localities was sometimes extreme.

THE STRENGTH OF EMPIRES
Comparative extent of major empires
in square miles and duration in years

There is no neat statistical way of comparing the power of the great empires. In general, empires are regarded as mighty because of both their expanse and their longevity. One non-scientific way of comparing them is by combining each one's duration and its size at its greatest extent into a single perspective.

extent:
14,157,000
sq. miles

duration:
390 years

extent:
7,500,000
sq. miles

duration:
480 years

extent:
12,800,000
sq. miles

duration:
200 years

extent:
1,540,000
sq. miles

duration:
1,150 years

extent:
2,160,000
sq. miles

duration:
640 years

extent:
4,863,000
sq. miles

duration:
360 years

extent:
2,200,000
sq. miles

duration:
510 years

extent:
1,425,000
sq. miles

duration:
330 years

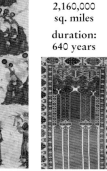

Roman Empire	Byzantine Empire	Mongol Empire	Ottoman Empire	Spanish Empire	Mogul Empire	British Empire	French Empire
31 BCE – CE 476	305 – 1453	1206 – 1405	c. 1281 – 1922	1492 – 1975	1526 – 1857	1583 – 1971	1605 – 1962

Yet the Ottoman Empire was also characterized by an extraordinary degree of cosmopolitanism and showed relative tolerance to its diverse population. Compared to the Europe of religious wars and pogroms, tax discrimination against Jews and Christians in the Ottoman Empire was a modest and tolerable form of second-class citizenship. The right existed to hold religious beliefs that were different from those of the ruler. This revealed an approach that, though inconsistently applied, was in principle centuries ahead of the European standard of the day.

In these two aspects of Ottoman power can be seen important features of the Empire's lasting impact on the Middle East. The very fact of the Empire helped maintain the Middle East as a single region, united along overlapping axes of language, religion, government, education and cultural assumptions. Within this unity, the Empire also fostered the region's diversity and complexity. Minority groups, including religious minorities, could find a reasonably comfortable place within it. Unlike Europe, which went through a century of warfare and barbarism in the struggle between the Catholic and Protestant versions of Christianity, the Ottoman Empire allowed different forms of Islam to coexist relatively peaceably. In many ways, the Greek Orthodox Church received more prestige and authority under the Muslim Ottoman Empire in its prime than ever under the Christian Byzantine Empire.

In the 18th and 19th centuries, the Empire faced the challenge of Wahhabism in the Arabian peninsula – a movement based on the demand for a return to early Islamic values and principles – and in response increased emphasis was placed on the religious role of the Sultan as Caliph. Even then, the Empire remained tolerant of religious difference.

At the same time, the form of government power that was bequeathed to the region – and perhaps more importantly, the culture of power – was arbitrary, aloof and capable of despotic repression of dissent. Despite the widespread appeal of democratic principles since the late 19th century, the archetypal and most common form of power in the Middle East remains arbitrary.

As a result, Middle Eastern states are ill-suited to meeting new challenges by steady adaptation, and reform programmes, when attempted, are inorganic. They are not driven by the needs of the ordinary people and cannot be genuinely innovative. This leads to frustration of popular demands and radicalization of popular movements, against which the elites resort to their old ways.

The economic dilemmas that the Middle East has faced and been unable to resolve – the high degree of illiteracy, the inability or unwillingness in most cases to use oil wealth for the general well-being, the uncertainty about how to face the modern world and challenges such as the empowerment of women – in part, these can be traced back to the lasting influence of one of world history's greatest Empires.

REMAINS OF THE OTTOMAN EMPIRE
Country names and borders 2008

territory remaining in 1914

19

EUROPEAN COLONIALISM

The long decline of the Ottoman Empire opened the door for the rising force of Europe to push its way into the Middle East. To begin with the pressure was almost surreptitious; it was hard to recognize and it was not part of a strategy for weakening the Empire but for gaining a tiny share of its fabulous wealth.

In the 16th century, special trading rights and tariff concessions granted to foreign governments – known as 'capitulations' – were initially an indication of Ottoman power. The poorer West came to the Sultan to seek special permission to trade. But the system meant that profitable trade increasingly fell into Western hands and by the 19th century, the capitulations were both a cause and a symptom of the Empire's economic weakness and its inability to modernize in the face of the European challenge. Increasingly during the 19th century, European trading and financial strength was not simply overwhelming the Ottoman grip on its peripheral regions, but weakening its economic core.

After trade came raw power. Suleiman the Magnificent had been baulked outside Vienna in the 1530s. A later Caliph was defeated 150 years later in the same place and the Empire's European dominions began to contract. A further century later, a French force landed in Egypt as an outgrowth of a western European war and batted aside a much larger Egyptian force, bringing to an end six centuries of power held by the Mamluks, who controlled Egypt but were subject to the Ottomans. Napoleon Bonaparte's Egyptian victory was tarnished by the arrival of a British fleet that destroyed his supply system and cut short his Middle East venture. Were it not for that, the consequences of Bonaparte's victory might have been more lasting.

As it was, Bonaparte not only brushed aside the Mamluks but smashed the image of Ottoman superiority. This was a decisive blow to Ottoman self-confidence and capacity to exercise far-flung power – and by the same token, a fillip to western European self-confidence and ability to win local allies.

On the back of trade and military superiority came – selectively at first, more or less comprehensively in the end – the urge to influence, control and rule. Through a combination of treaty agreements with local elites and military presence, the web of European influence and control spread. Algeria was the first major territory to come under direct European occupation, but further to the east the British were already nibbling at the fringes of Ottoman territory in the Arabian pensinsula.

That reflected a basic geostrategic pattern of European colonial expansion. The British emphasis was in the eastern half of the region, the French in the west. Not until after World War I – when France's rights as an ally were hard even for the British government to deny –

was France able to gain direct control of formerly Ottoman territories outside North Africa, though it had pressed for influence in modern-day Lebanon and Syria for much of the 19th century.

Britain's economic and strategic interests in the region were intensified by the opening of the Suez Canal – designed by a French engineer – which allowed the world's largest empire to achieve a quicker trade link with India and the rest of its Asian possessions. Following World War I, with its gains from the collapsed Ottoman Empire (as well as gains in Africa and Asia at the expense of defeated Germany), the British Empire reached its greatest extent, just as it entered a war-weary, economically broken period of unprecedented weakness.

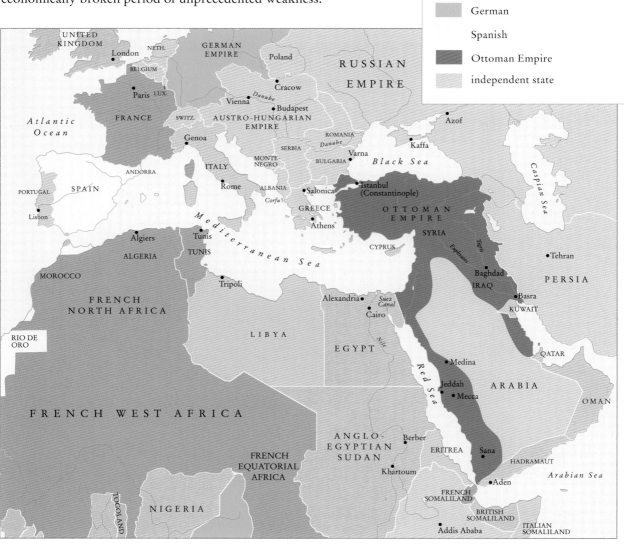

COLONIAL POWER AND THE OTTOMAN EMPIRE ON THE EVE OF WWI
Country names and borders 1914

- British
- French
- Italian
- German
- Spanish
- Ottoman Empire
- independent state

COLONIAL IMPACT

The name of the system of control was different in different places. A treaty of protection could be interpreted creatively to give the outside power decisive control over a state's internal affairs. Protectorate status could precede or ensue from direct military occupation. After World War I when, to meet American sensibilities, it was impolitic to bandy around terms such as 'imperial' and 'colonial', British and French power in formerly Ottoman territories was endorsed by a mandate from the League of Nations. The reality was colonial, whatever the name. Indeed, in Egypt, nominal independence in 1922 was completely consistent with continuing British control of everything it most valued. When World War II came, British control expanded to encompass the whole of Egypt, in case Egyptians might not automatically take the British side.

In general, compared to the British, French colonial power attempted to reach deeper into the fabric of the society and culture of the people it sought to dominate. The British sought to protect their strategic interests with as little intrusion as possible into the societies whose acquiescence they demanded. French colonial authorities both encouraged more French settlers and did more to attempt to reconstruct parts of Arab society into a French model. In Algeria, this included insistence on French schooling and compulsory military service. Opposition was ruthlessly suppressed. The 1871–72 Kabyle rebellion was a major uprising involving over 100,000 insurgent fighters, after which land seizure and denial of legal rights were used to punish and control the Algerian population. Despite these differences, the British authorities in Egypt likewise had no compunction in asserting their will. Notoriously in 1906, a fight involving five British army officers who were out hunting led to 32 Egyptians being convicted of premeditated murder: four were hanged and the rest were flogged.

Throughout the 19th century and even after they were allies from the beginning of the 20th century, Britain and France were imperial rivals in Africa and the Middle East. Each sought to gain territory before the other could, risking an armed clash as late as 1898 in southern Sudan, for example. As the Ottoman Empire weakened they manoeuvred against each other, mutually determined to keep other powers out, and especially Russia, each trying to concede the other as little as possible. As they picked at the pieces of the Ottoman Empire, Germany took a position of advantage in Istanbul, provided copious military assistance and gained an ally for World War I.

The deepest similarity between British and French colonialism in their respective Middle Eastern territories was the contradictory content and impact of what they brought with them from their western European homelands. The power of the new colonial masters was every bit as arbitrary as that of the Ottoman Empire. It was in no whit based on popular consent, though in both the British and French colonial elites there were those who prided themselves on knowing Arab society, knowing what Arabs wanted and needed, and knowing individual Arabs who would agree with the colonial diagnosis and treatment. As the years of colonial dominion wore on, the threadbare nature of those pretensions was ever more sharply exposed as colonial power met increasingly fierce resistance.

But arbitrary power was not the full story of the colonial impact. Britain and France both brought modernity into the Middle East, which came in the form of the products of the industrial age – not least, to begin with, greater wealth and superior military technology. It also came in the form of a modern way of thinking that emphasized organization, efficiency, discipline and the importance of achieving concrete results in every endeavour. Even while modernity continued to upturn old ways of life in Europe, it was being exported with profoundly destabilizing effects. Among Arab thinkers it initiated a long, and in many ways still unresolved, debate about how the Arab ways of life, the Arab identity and Islam could survive against modernity: was the best strategy to accept modernity, to confront it head on and reject it, or to attempt to co-opt and use those components of modern thinking that were not incompatible with Arab culture and religion?

Modernity, in short, was simultaneously troubling and tempting, made even more so by the third aspect of the West's contradictory impact – liberal and progressive political philosophy that stressed liberty, individual human rights and, by widely accepted extension, independence from colonial rule. These were not necessarily the views of even a small fraction of those Europeans who came to the Middle East in service of colonial government or for trade. And even those Europeans, whether living and working in the Middle East or back home, who did hold progressive political views in domestic matters – such as the extension of voting rights to all adults – did not necessarily believe such views applied to Arabs as well as Westerners.

But selectiveness and inconsistency could not mask the fact that the authority exerted by the colonial powers abroad was of a type that was, as time passed, increasingly unacceptable at home. In the period between World Wars I and II the right to hold colonies became a matter of political controversy in Europe in a way that had been unknown in the early days of their empires. And this philosophical uncertainty became increasingly visible in the Middle East and increasingly encouraging to those who sought independence, and who challenged the Western power on the basis, in part, of Western ideas of freedom.

THE NEW MIDDLE EAST AFTER WORLD WAR I

World War I was not only a war of unprecedented devastation and global reach, it also re-shaped world politics. It was born out of rivalry between the great European empires, and detonated by the particular rivalries in the Balkans – as great and medium powers fought to capitalize on the opportunities created by the culmination of the long Ottoman decline. War shattered three empires (Germany, Austria-Hungary and the Ottoman Empire itself), re-moulded one through revolution, civil war and terror as a new form of dictatorship (Russia), and exhausted two – Britain and France, who were the victors along with the USA and other allies, including Italy.

The peace settlement after the war was made up of a series of conferences and treaties that divided up the defeated powers' territories both in their homelands and their empires. Some of this re-alignment process created new states, some allotted control of extra territory to neighbouring states or to greater powers. This diplomacy continued for four years, from 1919 to 1923.

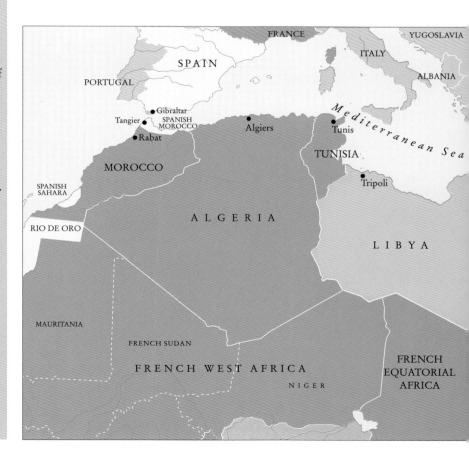

Faced with the slow weakening of the Ottoman Empire during the 19th century, it had been British policy to ensure that no other power gained a decisive advantage from the process. Early in World War I, the balance of British policy swung from stopping others gaining an advantage, to moving decisively to gain the regional advantage for itself.

In the course of this, the British government started to make promises, beginning in 1915, when it agreed to a special French role in the area of modern-day Lebanon and Syria. Between 1915 and 1916 it promised Hussein, the Sharif of Mecca, support for the establishment of an Arab kingdom in exchange for a revolt against the Ottomans. The kingdom was to stretch from the Indian Ocean in the south-east to what is today the northern border of Iraq, with the exception of the Syrian/Lebanese coast, the Holy Places in Palestine, and with special access for Britain to key points such as Baghdad and Basra *(see map page 32)*. Finally, in 1917, the British government promised to the British Zionist movement, and through it to the world movement, support for establishing a national Jewish home in Palestine.

(see map page 32)

CHRONOLOGY *continued*

1922 Anglo-Iraqi treaty leaves Iraq in control of its own affairs subject to overriding British control.
Greek forces defeated and withdraw from Turkey – Turkish Grand National Assembly abolishes the Ottoman Sultanate.

1923 Treaty of Lausanne sets boundaries of modern Turkey and supersedes the Treaty of Sèvres. Proclamation of the Republic of Turkey with Mustafa Kemal named President.

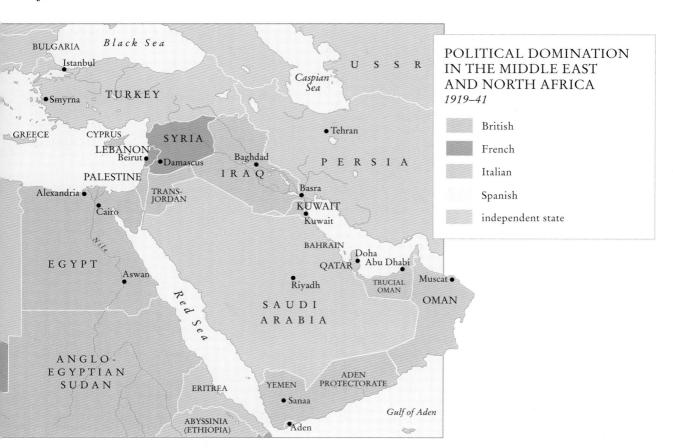

POLITICAL DOMINATION IN THE MIDDLE EAST AND NORTH AFRICA *1919–41*

British / French / Italian / Spanish / independent state

25

These promises could not all be fulfilled. They were made amid the exigencies of a war from which it was far from certain that Britain would emerge victorious. The historical record appears to indicate that it was the promise to the Arab leaders that was the most shallow. In a six-week period at the end of 1915 and the start of 1916, Britain and France negotiated an outline agreement – the Sykes-Picot agreement – on their shares of the spoils to come. France was 'given' control of a significant area of Anatolia and the eastern Mediterranean coastline, and influence in the northern and north-western parts; this included areas already promised to Hussein, Sharif of Mecca, by the British. Meanwhile, Britain took control in most of the rest of the promised Arab kingdom, including the Gulf coast, leaving the rest of the Arabian peninsula, except Aden, for the Arabs. Though the eventual map of the region was different from what the agreement envisaged, Sykes-Picot set the framework for both British and French policy for the new order in the Middle East.

The assumption behind these agreements was that, once the war was won, the victors would have it within their power to divide up Ottoman territory as they wished. However, the diplomatic process was more complex than the British or the French had foreseen. They were not the only players – as well as the rising power of the USA, there were the interests of Italy, who joined the Allies in 1915, and Greece to consider. Italy received some the Dodecanese Islands in the Aegean and Greece gained control of what territory it could in the traditional Hellenic areas of south-western Anatolia.

This imperial assumption by Britain and France appears to have been buttressed by a genuine belief that their rule would not only be good for Arabs but also popular. While British officials were accurately scathing about French expectations of a unanimous welcome from the Arabs who would come under the latter's dominion, they retained parallel delusions about their own popularity. Whenever and wherever it was possible to gauge Arab opinion, the preferred option was Arab rule.

The most important immediate constraint upon British and French plans after the war was fatigue. In the Middle East, the two European powers took on new imperial roles they no longer had the capacity to fulfil. Britain was unable to run Iraq and by 1922 opted instead to allow autonomy in its internal affairs and to establish a friendly king; the same arrangement was made in Egypt. The carve-up of Anatolia foreseen in the Sykes-Picot agreement never happened and, with British forces in the Middle East region rapidly shrinking after the end of the war, the decisive leadership of Mustafa Kemal drove out the Greek forces and constructed a new republic. Nor was it possible for Britain and France to maintain the commitment of the 1920 Treaty of Sèvres to give part of Anatolia to the proposed new state of Kurdistan; again, Mustafa Kemal's forces prevailed.

With grand plans, inadequate forces, and a lofty disdain for the people's will, Britain and France set out to impose a new regional order. The post-war settlement after World War I – while it actually left almost nothing settled – created the basic system of states and state borders that continues to shape the region's political geography today.

Negotiations between Britain and France over the partition of the Ottoman Empire took six weeks, starting in late November 1915.

British negotiations were led by Sir Mark Sykes. Widely travelled in the Middle East, especially Turkey, he gained the confidence of the British War Minister, Lord Kitchener, and dominated the government committee that in 1915 worked out British policy.

The French negotiations-leader was François Georges Picot, a foreign service official. His father and brother were influential figures in French policy in Africa and Asia respectively and he spoke for a combination of commercial, political and religious interests seeking a leading role in Lebanon and Syria.

The agreement was approved in early February 1916. It referred to the possibility of an independent Confederation of Arab states, but contradicted earlier promises made by Britain to the Sharif of Mecca.

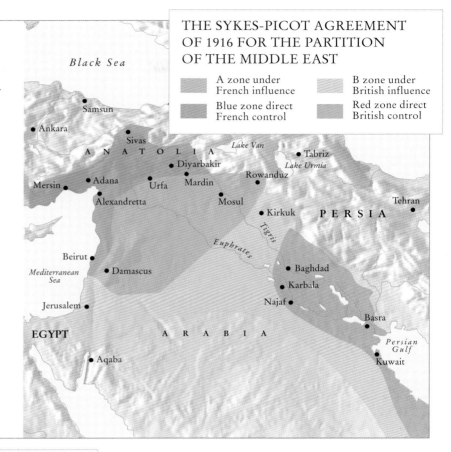

THE SYKES-PICOT AGREEMENT OF 1916 FOR THE PARTITION OF THE MIDDLE EAST

- A zone under French influence
- Blue zone direct French control
- B zone under British influence
- Red zone direct British control

THE STATE OF KURDISTAN
Proposed by Treaty of Sèvres *1920*

- proposed state
- to be given choice of joining after 1922

In parceling out the Ottoman Empire, Britain and France, the victorious powers, intended to create a Kurdish state. The Treaty of Sèvres fixed a two-stage process, with the Anatolian part given independence immediately and Iraqi Kurds being given the choice whether to join after 1922. For the new Turkey, Mustafa Kemal refused to cede any land and Britain and France backed down. In 1925, 25,000 died in a failed Kurdish uprising in Turkey.

DECOLONIZATION

European colonialism reached its zenith and began to decline at approximately the same time. While Britain and France emerged from World War I with more territory than ever – including significant gains in the Middle East – they also came out with less capacity for wielding power. While the era between the two world wars was superficially one of European dominance, the reality was that the colonial grip was beginning to slacken.

Developments in the Middle East unfolded within a larger context. Before World War I, Britain had already fought a bitter war to retain control in South Africa, and had then granted considerable autonomy to the white colonial class there and the other settler colonies of Australia, Canada and New Zealand. In Ireland it had faced the prospect of mutiny in the army before World War I over plans for partial independence, and the 1916 uprising was followed by the war of independence between 1919 and 1922. Meanwhile, in the Indian sub-continent – Britain's largest and most important imperial possession – the struggle for independence was intense throughout the inter-war period, culminating after World War II in 1947. Similar though less critical pressure was also felt almost throughout most of the French empire.

Thus, though both Britain and France had emerged from World War I as victors, they were not only weakened by the unprecedented human toll of the war and its economic costs, they were also facing multiple challenges to their power. At the same time the political climate in

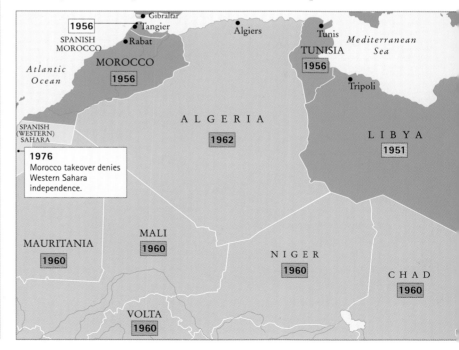

Europe was changing, weakening the self-confidence and unity of purpose necessary for the imperial enterprise.

This had already been reflected in the policy of not directly taking over formerly subject nations in Europe after World War I. Instead, the victors agreed to self-determination in the Balkans and central and eastern Europe. The inter-war years therefore provided considerable impetus for Arab nationalist sentiment and movements for independence.

World War II was another blow to the already weakening colonial system; if the human costs of war for Britain and France were not as great as in World War I, the economic and strategic costs were much greater. The two decades after 1945 were the era of decolonization – in the Middle East as everywhere. Under pressure throughout their empires, both quickly ceded power in the Levant – in France's case to Lebanon and Syria, and in Britain's case to Israel and Jordan. The colonial powers were also faced in the Middle East, more than in any other world region, by the rising power of the USA and the USSR. The region's traditional strategic importance, its contiguity with the southern borders of the USSR, and above all its oil, attracted the new global superpowers to seek to expand their influence in the Middle East. With all these factors in play, the end of the European colonial era was inevitable.

The imprint of colonialism

The colonial powers left their marks on the region's political geography. With the exception of Israel's expansion since independence and Yemen's unification, the boundaries bequeathed by colonialism have hardly changed. But in places such as Iraq, they are clearly unsuited to the needs and realities of the region and its people.

Britain and France left behind advances in education for limited sectors of the population. The emergent new middle class, associated with the government and military, became the driving force of the independence movements and, together with the traditional social elite, formed the basis of government in the new states.

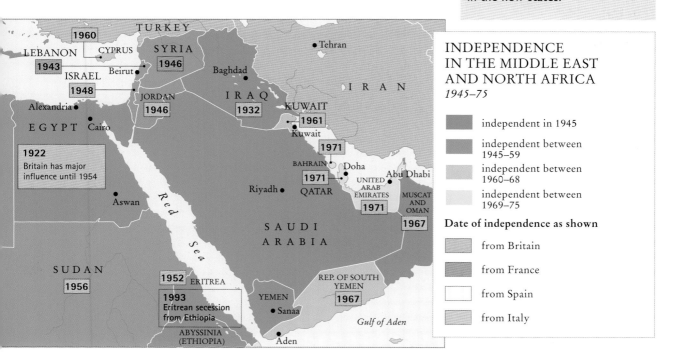

INDEPENDENCE
IN THE MIDDLE EAST
AND NORTH AFRICA
1945–75

- independent in 1945
- independent between 1945–59
- independent between 1960–68
- independent between 1969–75

Date of independence as shown

- from Britain
- from France
- from Spain
- from Italy

29

As Spain was abandoning the Western Sahara in 1976, Morocco disputed possession with Mauritania, and both faced opposition from the Polisario Front, which was founded in 1973, and which sought national independence. Morocco had asserted its claim in 1975 with the 'Green March' – a mobilization of over 300,000 people rallying at the border areas in the desert. Between 1975 and 1979, Mauritanian and Moroccan forces expelled tens of thousands of indigenous Sahrawi people who then fled to Algeria.

Mauritania withdrew its claims in 1979, and the territory it vacated was filled by Morocco, with an army that by the mid-1980s was about the same size as the Sahrawi population.

The fighting led to stalemate and in 1991 the UN brokered a cease-fire with a promise of a referendum among the Sahrawis. By 2006 the referendum had still not been held.

ANTI-COLONIAL FORCES

The decisive force in Egyptian nationalism after World War I was *al-Wafd al-Misrî*, meaning 'The Egyptian Delegation'. It was formed in November 1918, amid war-related high inflation and deteriorating living conditions, to send a delegation to London to discuss Egypt's post-war status. Its founder and leader was Sa'ad Zaghlul, a pre-war Minister of Justice and former high court judge. The British responded by arresting Zaghlul and exiled him and other *Wafd* members to Malta, a move that provoked a nationwide revolt in March 1919. The toll after three weeks of rioting was 800 Egyptians killed.

Zaghlul was released and presented the case for Egyptian independence at the Versailles peace conference. Although the *Wafd*'s demands were ignored, Zaghlul's negotiations with the British continued in 1920 and thereafter as unrest continued in Egypt.

In 1922, the British granted formal independence to Egypt as a constitutional monarchy but retained control over key government institutions and the Suez Canal. The *Wafd* became a political party in 1923, and in 1924 took 90 percent of the seats in the First Chamber and formed the government with Zaghlul as Prime Minister.

In World War II, the *Wafd* supported the allies on the understanding that Egypt would gain full independence once the war was over. Not surprisingly perhaps, the *Wafd* was blamed when the end of the war in 1945 did not lead to full independence and British armed forces remained in Egypt in strength. Even though the *Wafd* government in 1951 abrogated the 1936 treaty that gave Britain responsibility for the protection of foreign interests and the rights of national minorities, the party was now seen as incapable of bringing full independence. It was the 1952 coup by the Free Officers that took Egypt into fully independent statehood, and among the new government's early actions was the dissolution of the *Wafd*.

In Algeria, the National Liberation Front (FLN) was set up in 1954 with the explicit aim of gaining independence from France. It was created by the Revolutionary Committee of Unity and Action, which urged all the warring factions of the Algerian nationalist movement to unite against the French colonial power.

The FLN carried out its first attacks in November 1954, less than six months after French rule in South-East Asia had been ended by defeat at Dien Bien Phu in Vietnam. By the end of 1955, France had committed more than 400,000 troops to Algeria. Growing opposition to the war in Algeria emerged in France in the late 1950s and talks were opened in May 1961. The war ended in 1962 with a cease-fire agreement and an Algerian referendum approving independence.

Estimates of fatalities in the war range up to 1.5 million. Algeria had attracted large numbers of French settlers, making up approximately one-sixth of the population at its peak. There was extreme bitterness among settlers at what they perceived as abandonment by France, and the most militant fomented a failed mutiny in the French army and carried out violent acts of sabotage.

The FLN was the only legal political party in Algeria until the late 1980s, and was the largest party in parliament after the 2002 elections.

The Suez crisis

1954 April Two years after Free Officers' coup, Colonel Nasser assumes the position of Egyptian Prime Minister.

October Britain and Egypt agree timetable to evacuate the British Suez base.

1955 Escalation of Egypt-Israel conflict – Egypt blockades Straits of Tiran making Israel's port at Eilat unusable – Israeli military raids into Gaza.

East-West Cold War escalates in the Middle East. Iraq, Turkey, Britain, Pakistan and Iran form the Baghdad Pact for military strength against the USSR – Egypt begins to receive Soviet weapons via an arms deal with Czechoslovakia.

1956 March France calls on Egypt to end support for the Algerian FLN – Nasser refuses.

April UN Secretary-General starts process seeking to re-establish Israeli-Egyptian armistice.

June Nasser becomes President of Egypt after unopposed election. British withdrawal from the Suez Canal zone complete.

July Nasser nationalizes the Suez Canal Company. Britain and USA retaliate by withdrawing funding for Aswan Dam development project.

October Egypt, Syria and Jordan sign defence pact.
Britain, France and Israel finalize plan to act against Egypt.

29 October Israel attacks Egypt.

30 October Britain and France deliver ultimatum calling on parties to end fighting – as planned, Israel agrees – as expected, Egypt refuses. UN calls for cease-fire and withdrawal of Israeli forces.

31 October British and French forces bomb the Suez Canal zone. US President Eisenhower publicly condemns the use of force in the Middle East and threatens to use economic strength against Britain and France.

5 November USSR threatens to intervene with force if attacks on Egypt continue.

6 November British and French forces take control of Suez but the British Cabinet is informed that the value of the British currency is threatened and gold reserves have fallen by one-eighth in the attempt to protect the pound sterling against US pressure.

7 November End of the Suez War.

12 November Egypt agrees to deployment of a UN force in Canal zone.

22 November Last British troops leave the Canal zone.

1957 April Suez Canal re-opens for international commerce.

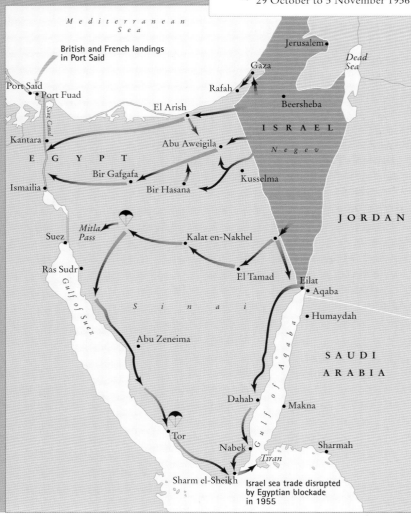

THE SINAI CAMPAIGN
October–November 1956

Israel 1948 to 1967

Israeli parachute landing troops

principal Israeli advances
29 October to 5 November 1956

ARAB NATIONALISM

As the Arab world sought independence from European colonial rule, some Arab thinkers and politicians envisaged a larger goal than independent statehood; a vision of pan-Arab unity.

For a century and a half from the time of Napoleon Bonaparte's defeat of the Mamluks in Egypt in 1798, the Middle East was confronted, challenged and, by many measures, bested by Europe. One answer to the overriding question of how the Arab world should respond to the challenge of western European power came in the form of anti-colonialism. But to be against colonial domination could not, neither in logic nor in political reality, be a matter only of opposing the existing dominant foreign power. It had to be also a statement – a political programme, in fact – of the better future that would be obtained through overthrowing colonial power. Despite some nostalgia for a different empire, by and large the anti-colonial movements did not seek a return to Ottoman rule; instead, they sought independence – a new state.

As movements for independence got going however, the pre-existing unity of the region began to influence political ideas and programmes. Though there are many differences among Arabs in different parts of the region – inevitably in such large and relatively thinly populated areas – there is also much that is shared in terms of language and culture, not least religion, history and experience. It is easy to exaggerate how much is shared; not all Arabs are Muslims, for example, and there are several different forms of Arabic, some of which are barely mutually comprehensible *(see page 114)*. There are also sharp rivalries and different interests among the Arab elites and, as everywhere, deep cleavages of class and sharp distinctions between urban and rural dwellers. Nonetheless, Arabs in different parts of the Middle East have mutual connections that are much stronger and more real than those to be found among, for example, Europeans in different parts of Europe. Moreover, advocates of Arab unity argued that, on top of everything else they shared, the Arab world also had a common enemy – the West.

ARAB KINGDOM PROMISED TO HUSSEIN BY THE BRITISH *1915–16*

Ideas of Arab unity spread during and immediately after World War I. One of their most famous proponents, though his ideas were not especially influential at the time, was the British army intelligence officer, TE Lawrence – Lawrence of Arabia. The Arab revolt in 1916, in which he played his role as a liaison officer and strategic adviser to the uprising, was a key moment in the evolution of the idea of unity. The leaders of the revolt were the Hashemite family, led by Hussein ibn Ali, the Sharif (religious leader) of Mecca, who had turned down approaches from the Young Turk government in Istanbul to take up arms against the British; his sons, Faisal and Abdullah, led the Arab forces in the field. To win the alliance, the British had promised Hussein he would have a new kingdom embracing most of the Arab world east of Egypt. This was a dynastic ambition Hussein could not have fulfilled by allying with Istanbul. As it turned out, the British broke their promises straight after the war, and instead of a large single state created a patchwork of smaller ones, though Hashemite leaders took power in Transjordan, Iraq and in the Arabian peninsula (where their grip on power was broken in 1925 by Ibn Saud, the founder of Saudi Arabia).

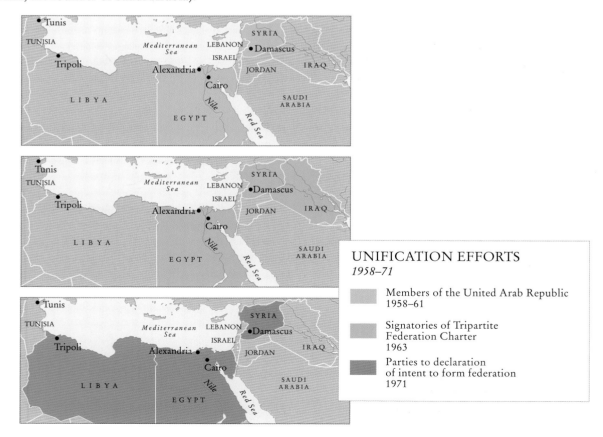

UNIFICATION EFFORTS
1958–71

Members of the United Arab Republic 1958–61

Signatories of Tripartite Federation Charter 1963

Parties to declaration of intent to form federation 1971

THE NEW PAN-ARAB MOVEMENT

As Arab leaders, the Hashemites had tradition and lineage – Hashemites had been Sharifs of Mecca since the 10th century – but their ambitions stretched only to the Levant and Arabia. The emergence of a popular nationalist political movement basing itself on the idea of Arab unity and claiming to speak for the Arab nation as a whole began to take a clear shape only after World War I. It grew in the context both of the weakness-within-strength of the European empires and the language of national self-determination that was current during the post-war peace conferences.

Pan-Arab nationalism is a political philosophy based on a cultural premise. Writing in the inter-war years, Sati al-Husri (1880–1968), a Syrian writer, was a particularly influential advocate of cultural Arab nationalism; his ideas found a more directly political form of expression in the writings, speeches and actions of Michel Aflaq (1910–89), also a Syrian, one of the key founders of the Ba'ath party in 1947. Aflaq advocated the formation of a single Arab state.

The high tide of pan-Arab nationalism came in the 1950s. Its advocates argued that the unity of the Arabs was a cultural fact; the defeats that the Arab world faced when divided provided some of the key motivation for recognizing and acting upon this claim of unity. A powerful argument for political unity lay in the inability of the Arab states to prevent the establishment of Israel in 1948, and in the defeat of the armies of five Arab states – Egypt, Iraq, Jordan, Lebanon and Syria – by the new state in 1948–49.

Onto this platform constructed by hope and defeat came a charismatic leader in the person of Gamal Abdel Nasser, leader of the Free Officers' coup in Egypt in 1952, Prime Minister from 1954, and President of Egypt from 1956. And it was above all the successful outcome of Nasser's decisive moves to force the British out of Egypt, to take the Suez Canal into Egyptian ownership, and finally to face down the combined strength of Britain, France and Israel in 1956 *(see map page 31)* that gave him the international credibility to be the voice and leader of pan-Arab aspirations for unity.

For many Arabs, Nasser's political and strategic daring and decisiveness formed a sharp and encouraging contrast to the caution and conservatism of their traditional leaders. Even though the favourable outcome of the Suez crisis in 1956 owed at least as much to US opposition to the adventurism of Britain and France, and accordingly to the economic pressure the USA exerted against Britain in particular, as it did to Egyptian obduracy, here at last was a victory against the European colonial powers and against Israel.

Two years after Suez, Arab unity was put into practice with the establishment of the United Arab Republic (UAR) in 1958 by Syria and Egypt. This was the pinnacle of pan-Arab nationalism. It should probably also be seen as the beginning of the end.

Great effort went into bringing the union about, but once it was achieved it lasted only three years, partly because Syrian politicians objected to what they experienced as Egyptian dominance and partly because there was no practical programme of action for the day after unity was achieved.

Two years later, Ba'athist coups in Syria and Iraq presaged another attempt at union – this time a federation of three states. This effort never got beyond an intention and a plan. Increasingly tense rivalry between Iraq and Syria, despite their common political party roots, meant that by the time a third effort at a union of Arab states was made in 1971, Iraq had dropped out and was replaced by Libya.

This third effort was little more than rhetorical. By then, as a practical political programme, pan-Arab nationalism was effectively a thing of the past. In 1967, Israel once again defeated a coalition of Arab states, and did so with devastating swiftness in only six days of war. The new Arab world, it seemed, for all its talk of unity, was in reality as weak as the old. Israel expanded its territory at the expense of Egypt, Jordan and Syria alike and could do so, it seemed, with impunity as the world community appeared either indifferent or pro-Israel. Three years after this crushing defeat, Nasser died and pan-Arab nationalism could be pronounced dead at the same time.

An attempt by the new Libyan leader, Colonel Muammar Qadhafi, to assume Nasser's mantle in more militant mode had little foundation in reality. Though Egypt and Syria were allies in a new war against Israel in 1973, which did not end in victory and yet was not the unqualified disaster that 1967 had been, the reality of Arab disunity was shown by the separate peace deal Egypt arrived at with Israel in the period from 1977 to 1979, and by the way Libya and Syria both sided with Iran against Iraq in the Iran-Iraq war starting in 1980.

The language of pan-Arab nationalism was deeply appealing to large numbers of Arabs, yet it was rarely matched in practice. There were disputes and tensions between the different governments, each with their own interests, and many Arab leaders saw the pan-nationalists as a revolutionary threat. There was war among Arabs when Egypt went to war in Yemen from 1962 to 1967. And there was conflict among Arabs again in 1990 when Iraq invaded Kuwait and Syria and Egypt joined Saudia Arabia and the Gulf states in the US-led coalition for war against Iraq in 1991.

The failure of Arab unity in practice has been profound – unity was achieved only for short periods, and even then it was never very effective (Suez, after all, was Egypt's achievement, not a general Arab success, widely though it was celebrated). Nonetheless, much of the sentiment behind pan-Arab nationalism remains important. It continues to have an important institutional vehicle in the Arab League, founded in 1945, even if the League's declarations do little more than remind Arabs of the long-term ineffectiveness of the project of unity.

Other ideologies were soon to fill the vaccum left by the demise of pan-Arabism.

THE FORMATION OF THE STATE OF ISRAEL

To the citizens of the new state, the declaration of Israel's independence on 14 May 1948 marked the realization of a dream and the creation of a place of survival and belonging after genocide. To Palestinians, the event is simply known as *al-nakba* – the catastrophe.

The term Zionism was coined by a Jewish writer a few years after the beginning, in 1882, of migration to historic Palestine by Jews with the goal not only of escaping anti-Jewish prejudice, discrimination and, at worst, pogroms, but also of ultimately establishing a homeland. Despite the political intention, the early migrations seemed innocuous and the numbers insignificant. Different population estimates show between 10,000 and 24,000 Jews living in the area later called Palestine in about 1880. Over the next three decades, perhaps as many as 1,000 Jews arrived each year. By the end of World War I, some estimates put the Jewish population as numbering about 56,000.

The meaning of this migration and its possible consequences only started to clarify during World War I as the Ottoman Empire went from decline to break-up. As plans were formulated to re-make the Middle East, and with the declaration in 1917 by British Foreign Secretary Arthur Balfour supporting 'the establishment in Palestine of a national home for the Jewish people,' Zionism became both more significant and realistic. Though the Zionist Organization's 1919 proposal for a Jewish homeland stretching well to the east of the Jordan river was flatly rejected by the great powers, the British government permitted continuing Jewish immigration into Palestine throughout the inter-war years. The British authorities did, however, make a sharp division between the areas to the west and to the east of the river, and in 1922 established Transjordan as a separate entity into which they refused to permit further Jewish immigration.

There were from time to time – both from British politicians and from

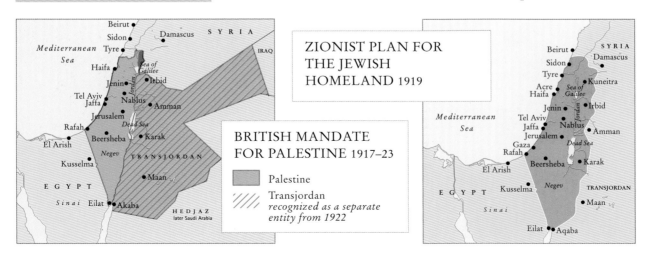

ZIONIST PLAN FOR THE JEWISH HOMELAND 1919

BRITISH MANDATE FOR PALESTINE 1917–23

Palestine

Transjordan *recognized as a separate entity from 1922*

Jewish leaders – statements that Jews and Arabs could and would live peacefully alongside each other. The 1917 Balfour Declaration included the 'understanding' that 'nothing shall be done which may prejudice the civil and religious rights of existing non-Jewish communities in Palestine'. But Zionists did not simply want a place for Jews to live; they wanted a Jewish state, and that made hopes of easy peaceful cooperation unrealistic. 1920 saw the first Arab violence against Jewish immigrants and the first organized Jewish response. In 1929 came anti-Jewish riots. In 1936, as Jewish immigration increased after Hitler's 1933 assumption of power in Germany and the anti-semitic policies of the Nazis, a major Arab uprising began, lasting until 1939. It was aimed equally against British rule and growing Zionist encroachment; particular causes of resentment were the willingness of the immigrants to pay any price for land – well above reasonable market values – and the willingness of some Arab landowners to sell, enriching themselves while weakening the position of the Palestinian community.

The British authorities suppressed the uprising and attempted to forestall a violent Jewish response and the spiral of escalation that would ensue. They also responded by studying – some 20 years after the initial commitment to creating a Jewish homeland – how this could be done. Successive Royal Commissions in 1937 and 1938 examined the question and produced proposals for partition – a two-state solution, one for the Arabs and one for the Jews.

By the late 1930s there were about 400,000 Jews in Palestine, in a population of about 1.3 million. It was no longer possible to dismiss the inflow as insignificant. It was also well understood, at least by the British authorities, that the arrival of Jews and the possible establishment of a new state was opposed by most Palestinians, and that Palestinians had no reason to think they could thrive or even co-exist in a Jewish state.

CHRONOLOGY *continued*

1939–45 World War II. Mass murder of Jews in Europe.

1946 Jewish militants blow up the King David Hotel, Jerusalem killing 91.

1947 February Britain refers Palestine issue to the United Nations.

November UN votes for partition of Palestine into separate Jewish and Palestinian states with special international status for Jerusalem. Internal violence starts.

1948

14 May State of Israel proclaimed.

15 May First Arab-Israeli War.

1949 War ends – Israel becomes member of the UN – Knesset and the Israeli government move to Jerusalem.

1950 West Bank officially annexed by Jordan.

1964 Palestine Liberation Organization (PLO) established.

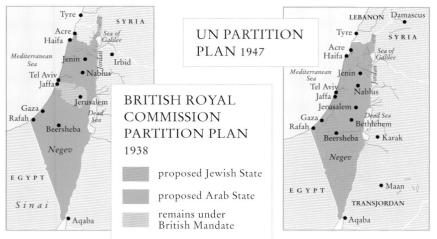

UN PARTITION PLAN 1947

BRITISH ROYAL COMMISSION PARTITION PLAN 1938

proposed Jewish State

proposed Arab State

remains under British Mandate

ISRAEL'S BORDERS 1949

ZIONISM AND ANTI-SEMITISM

From 1948 until 1973, the Jewish population of Israel increased from about 657,000 to over 3 million; more than half of the population increase (over 1.3 million out of 2.4 million) was directly accounted for by immigration from at least 30 countries. In all of these countries, Jews had been minorities, and how they lived – not least the degree of prejudice and discrimination they faced, but also many other facets of their daily lives – was shaped in part by their interactions with the majority communities. Though united by being Jewish and in many cases by having experienced persecution, they were also a highly diverse population, from different cultural backgrounds, speaking different languages, and brought up in different education systems. Out of this diversity, in a hostile environment, the new state of Israel set about building an Israeli nation.

Education, the projection of national symbols, the development of a historical narrative culminating in the establishment of the new state, the teaching of a new national language – all these standard tools of modern nation-building have been deployed by Israel. The identification of the establishment of Israel with the fulfilment of a religious mission adds a further dimension and greater depth to nation-building than has been available to most new states of the post-1945 era. That both the original dream of a homeland and the eventual establishment of the new state grew from persecution, and that the persecution of Jews in 20th-century Europe reached unprecedented depths of violence, together with the

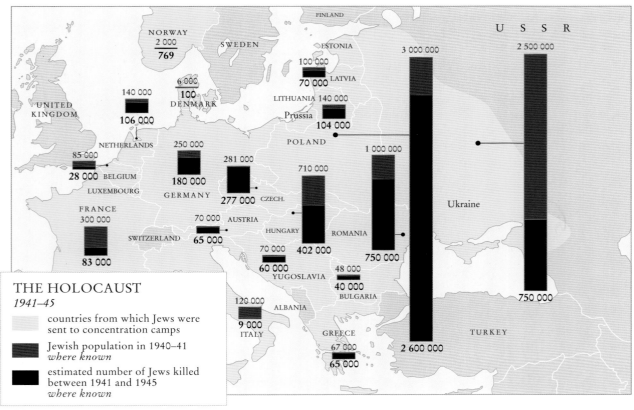

THE HOLOCAUST
1941–45

- countries from which Jews were sent to concentration camps
- Jewish population in 1940–41 *where known*
- estimated number of Jews killed between 1941 and 1945 *where known*

violence and hostility amid which Israel was established, have all contributed to the instance within Israel that nationality is of paramount importance. And the continuing experience of hostility from the Arab world after 1948 – though not uniform – makes the maintenance of national security a definitive part of national identity.

Considerably before Israel's foundation, the ideas of Ze'ev Jabotinsky became influential among the first generation of Israel's leaders. In articles written in 1923, Jabotinsky dismissed optimistic arguments that the Arabs would accept and even support the establishment of the homeland for Jews and argued that an 'Iron Wall' had to be built, based on military strength, to enforce and defend statehood until Palestinian resistance to the fact had broken down. Once Palestinians accepted the reality of Israel's existence, negotiations could begin and a pragmatic compromise could be worked out. Until that point, in Jabotinsky's view, Israel should be uncompromisingly reliant on its own strength.

The Palestine Liberation Organization, internationally accepted as speaking for the Palestinian people, recognized Israel's sovereignty over 78 percent of historical Palestine in 1988. To most observers, that seemed to mean the goal of the Iron Wall strategy had been achieved. The very mixed history of Israeli-Palestinian negotiations since then suggests that the transition out of the Iron Wall strategy has been much less straightforward than Jabotinsky had assumed.

Zionism

Over the years Zionism has displayed some striking dualities – a secular ideology that came to be buttressed in deeply religious fashion, an ideology that is as liberating for some as it is profoundly threatening for others. Only by pretending that Jews did not experience brutal persecution is it possible to deny Zionism's liberatory aspect; only by denying that Palestinians have human rights is it possible to ignore the threatening aspect of the same ideology.

JEWISH MIGRATION TO THE NEW ISRAEL
1948–early 1970s

country of origin and number of Jewish migrants *rounded to 500*

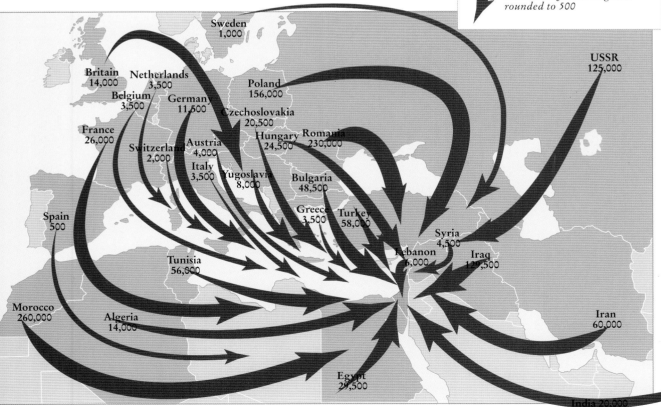

Sweden 1,000
USSR 125,000
Britain 14,000
Netherlands 3,500
Poland 156,000
Belgium 3,500
Germany 11,500
Czechoslovakia 20,500
France 26,000
Hungary 24,500
Romania 230,000
Switzerland 2,000
Austria 4,000
Italy 3,500
Yugoslavia 8,000
Bulgaria 48,500
Spain 500
Greece 3,500
Turkey 58,000
Syria 4,500
Lebanon 6,000
Iraq 129,500
Tunisia 56,000
Morocco 260,000
Algeria 14,000
Iran 60,000
Egypt 29,500
India 20,000

FLIGHT AND EXILE

Palestinians are the largest group of refugees in the world today; a total of more than 4 million are officially registered with the UN Relief and Works Agency (UNRWA) as refugees and the number grows at a rate of about 3 percent each year, approximately an additional 120,000 people. Of the total about a third, 1.3 million, live in 59 refugee camps in Jordan, Lebanon, Syria, Gaza and the West Bank *(see map page 137)*.

The first wave of flight came with the foundation of Israel in 1948. It began with the fighting that started as soon as the UN voted for partition in November 1947. During the war in 1948, over 400 Palestinian villages were cleared and destroyed – nearly half of all Palestinian villages in Mandatory Palestine at the time. In all, over 80 percent of Palestinians living within the borders of Israel left. The second major outflow of refugees came in 1967 when Israel took control of the West Bank.

Over the years there have been fierce controversies about why the Palestinians left between 1947 and 1949, with some claiming that they did so largely on orders from their political leaders, more to make a political point than out of fear for their lives. Others have claimed that, whatever the reasons for leaving, they have been kept in refugee camps, instead of integrating into the surrounding Arab countries, in order to make a point and to sustain the argument for their return to Israel.

Detailed studies have been done based on official archives. These show very few cases in which specific orders by Arab leaders to abandon villages can be traced. Cases in which instructions were given, even when combined with those where the motive for flight is uncertain, account for less than 20 percent of all villages abandoned. In 80 percent or more of cases, the motives were that Israeli forces cleared the villagers out, or the village came under attack, or that the villagers were influenced by what happened down the road in another village, or that they were afraid of being caught up in the fighting, or that they were influenced by a whispering campaign, mounted by the Israel Defence Force and the Haganah group, aimed at stoking Palestinian fears.

Israel rejects the right of 'return' for the refugees and displaced persons. Israel wants to solve the problem with a mixture of resettlement in Arab countries, international efforts to improve the

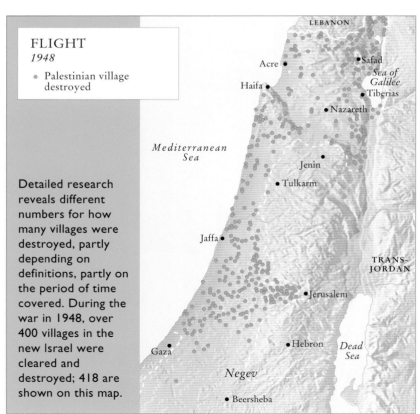

FLIGHT
1948
- Palestinian village destroyed

Detailed research reveals different numbers for how many villages were destroyed, partly depending on definitions, partly on the period of time covered. During the war in 1948, over 400 villages in the new Israel were cleared and destroyed; 418 are shown on this map.

LEBANON

Acre • · Safad
Sea of Galilee
Haifa • · Tiberias
• Nazareth

Mediterranean Sea

Jenin •
• Tulkarm

Jaffa •

TRANS-JORDAN

• Jerusalem

• Hebron · *Dead Sea*

Gaza •

Negev

• Beersheba

refugees' living conditions, and restricted re-admission. The Palestine Liberation Organization insists on the absolute right of return for all Palestinian refugees of 1948. Many neutral observers have agreed over the years that the best short-to-medium term interests of Palestinian refugees themselves sometimes take second place to the political manoeuvring for this longer-term goal.

From the beginning of the 20th century to its end, the situation of the Palestinian people underwent a shattering transformation, as they went from being the well-established inhabitants of a region with family ties going back generations, to dispersal into a diaspora. This transformation unfolded because of, and at the same time as, the relocation of large numbers of Jews in their diaspora to Palestine, which was itself the result of what had been suffered by Jewish communities over centuries, culminating in an unparalleled holocaust. The response to these historical traumas has been to set group against group, placing an iron divide between them, thus germinating new agonies in the region.

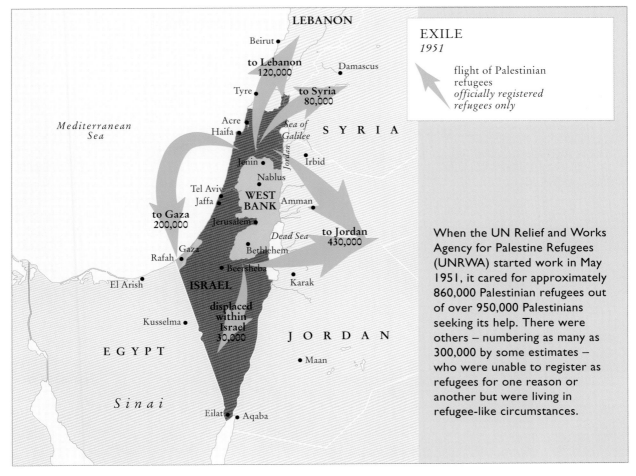

EXILE
1951

flight of Palestinian refugees
officially registered refugees only

When the UN Relief and Works Agency for Palestine Refugees (UNRWA) started work in May 1951, it cared for approximately 860,000 Palestinian refugees out of over 950,000 Palestinians seeking its help. There were others — numbering as many as 300,000 by some estimates — who were unable to register as refugees for one reason or another but were living in refugee-like circumstances.

OIL

Crude oil is the world's most actively traded commodity. It lies at the heart of transport and therefore of world manufacturing and the production and distribution of food. About 68 percent of the world's proven oil reserves lie in the Middle East, almost all in the Gulf region.

Oil was discovered in Iran before World War I by British interests. There was a surge of oil discovery during the 1930s and the tempo of commercial exploitation picked up in the decade after World War II. Saudi Arabia's annual income from oil production before World War II was about half a million dollars; by 1950 it was over $50 million and five years later was rising above $200 million.

The control of these vast, economically crucial natural resources capable of generating mega-profits was a sensitive issue from the beginning of significant exploitation. In Iran, Mohammed Mossadeq became Prime Minister in 1951 with a programme of taking Iranian oil exploitation into Iranian ownership. Two years later, after considerable instability and a British boycott, Mossadeq was ousted in a coup set up by the CIA with British intelligence assistance. The issue, however, would not go away.

In 1959, Western oil companies cut world prices, thus reducing the income of producing states. In response, the Organization of Petroleum Exporting Countries (OPEC) was established the following year by several Middle East states – including Iraq, Iran, Kuwait and Saudi

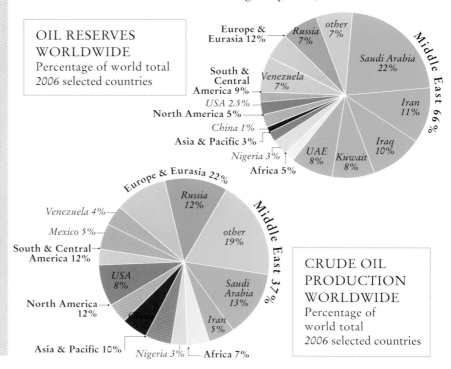

OIL RESERVES WORLDWIDE
Percentage of world total
2006 selected countries

Europe & Eurasia 12%
Russia 7%
other 7%
Saudi Arabia 22%
South & Central America 9%
Venezuela 7%
Iran 11%
USA 2.5%
North America 5%
China 1%
Asia & Pacific 3%
Nigeria 3%
Iraq 10%
Africa 5%
UAE 8%
Kuwait 8%
Middle East 66%

Europe & Eurasia 22%
Russia 12%
other 19%
Venezuela 4%
Mexico 5%
South & Central America 12%
Saudi Arabia 13%
USA 8%
North America 12%
China 5%
Iran 5%
Asia & Pacific 10%
Nigeria 3%
Africa 7%
Middle East 37%

CRUDE OIL PRODUCTION WORLDWIDE
Percentage of world total
2006 selected countries

Arabia – and Venezuela. For the duration of the 1960s, the new oil cartel could not affect world prices. Things began to change when the Suez Canal was closed as a result of the Six Day War in 1967 and not reopened until the disengagement accord of 1973. Libya's geographic position, west of the Canal, gave it an advantage in terms of the convenience of its supplies as the Canal's closure did not disrupt its oil routes. Libya negotiated higher oil prices with a group of US oil companies that were smaller than, and independent of, the giant transnational corporations that dominated world trade. Iran, Iraq and Saudi Arabia all managed to follow suit and in 1971 a general deal was made – the Tehran agreement – setting prices for the next five years.

But in October 1973, with the new Arab-Israeli War, OPEC became not only an economic but also a political instrument. Now accustomed to working closely together, Middle Eastern oil states agreed to reduce supplies, cutting them altogether to countries whose governments supported Israel, and to raise prices. When the war was over and sanctions lifted, prices increased nonetheless, quadrupling in a single year. Oil income rose dramatically – from half a billion dollars to $7 billion in two years for Iraq, and from $2.7 billion to $25 billion for Saudi Arabia.

In relation to Middle Eastern oil, issues of control, access and influence are now fundamental to world politics. This places the Middle East in the centre of world politics and keeps outside powers' interests a key force in shaping events in the region. As long as oil is important in advanced economies, this will not change – except by becoming more marked in coming decades. Even though proved reserves have increased by almost 60 percent since the early 1980s, the fact that the Middle East's share of proved oil reserves is about twice as high as its share of annual production means its prominence in oil production will endure.

CHRONOLOGY *continued*

1990 August Iraq invades Kuwait; world oil prices soar.
1991 January USA offensive against Iraq – oil prices fall. Post-war UN economic sanctions against Iraq.
1992 UN sanctions against Libya.
1995 UN 'Oil-For-Food' programme controls sale of Iraqi oil to buy essentials; later revealed to be corrupt.
2000 Oil prices rise following attack on the USS Cole in Aden harbour.
2002 US Congress authorizes President Bush to use force if necessary against Iraq on grounds of its alleged weapons of mass destruction programme.
2003 US war on Iraq with Britain, Australia and some other states participating – Saddam Hussein overthrown, occupation begins, resistance starts. UN ends economic sanctions against Iraq. UN sanctions against Libya lifted.
2004 Insurgents in Iraq attack the country's oil infrastructure.
2005 Oil prices at an all-time high due to war in Iraq and Hurricane Katrina in the USA.

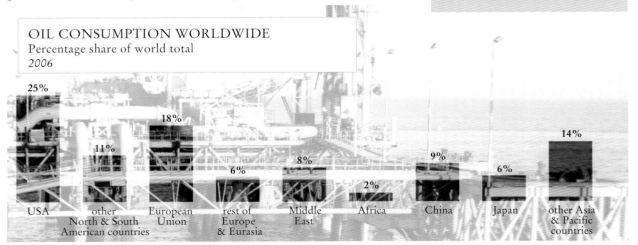

OIL CONSUMPTION WORLDWIDE
Percentage share of world total
2006

25% USA
11% other North & South American countries
18% European Union
6% rest of Europe & Eurasia
8% Middle East
2% Africa
9% China
6% Japan
14% other Asia & Pacific countries

Transport and choke points

Each day about 43 million barrels (about 5 million metric tons) of crude oil are transported by sea. About 35 million barrels per day are taken through relatively narrow shipping lanes and through pipelines. Strategic concerns about the vulnerability of these choke points are a constant background theme in the tangled international political positioning and manoeuvring on Middle Eastern issues. The concerns once focused on the potential for action by governments – whether of the region or further afield – that might want to strangle oil supplies to, for example, Western Europe or Japan in time of crisis. Recently, the focus of concern has shifted as some non-state groups have demonstrated the capacity to make spectacularly destructive attacks on very high profile targets. Were such attacks to occur, the jittery nature of world oil markets means prices would almost certainly rise, at least for a period, with knock-on economic effects.

After the sharp rise in oil prices in 1973 to 1974 and at the end of the 1970s, prices fell just as quickly in the first half of the 1980s, and were even lower for most of the 1990s. In normal times, oil producing states do not want exorbitant prices, both because it is in their interests that the world economy grows, and because they want no economic incentives for rich countries to start developing alternative forms of energy for transport. They want high revenues, and their positions were hurt by declining prices in the 1980s but they would suffer more if they raised long-term prices too much.

Oil prices rose from 2000 in a market response to regional instability. First came the Palestinian uprising against Israeli occupation in September 2000. Then came the increased focus on terrorist groups with roots in the Middle East after September 2001. Finally, the USA invaded Iraq in 2003 and resistance and mayhem ensued.

In debates in western Europe and the USA about the 1991 war on Iraq, it was said more than once that if Kuwait's and Iraq's main natural resource were carrots, there would be no war. It is a strong point, but it does not mean that US concern about its own oil supplies explains its reasons for going to war on Iraq in 1991 and 2003; the USA has covered itself against a repeat use of the oil weapon. In the early 1970s, US reliance on oil from the Middle East was increasing as its reliance on oil from the Americas fell. Events forced a re-think and determined action soon reversed the trends – US reliance on oil from the Americas rose from the late 1970s and reliance on Middle Eastern oil fell. Among the richest countries, it is Japan that is the most vulnerable to the oil weapon.

The USA's long-term interest is, like the oil producing states, in a smoothly functioning world economy. In 1990 when Saddam Hussein's Iraq occupied Kuwait, the fear was that the Iraqi dictator would then control 20 percent of the world's proved reserves. It would provide him, at key moments, with considerable bargaining power in regional and world politics, not because he could have stopped American cars from running, but because of the potential of widespread disruption of markets and consequent economic slowdown.

Oil is such a central commodity for the modern world, that it must always be a political issue. Shared usage of the Shatt al-Arab waterway – part of which is on the Iraq-Iran border, and through which Iran needs tanker

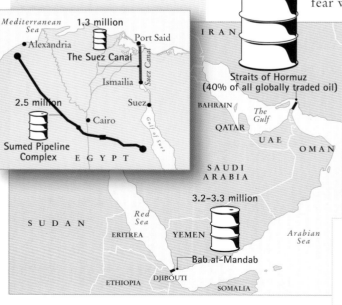

OIL ROUTES AND STRATEGIC CHOKE POINTS
2000–03

oil flows through key points millions of barrels per day

access in and out of its oil complex at Abadan – was at the heart of the Iran-Iraq War in the 1980s. The war was brutal and threatened to become a global conflict issue when Iran and Iraq each tried to disrupt the other's oil exports in the 'tanker war'. Oil infrastructure is also a natural target for attack, as Iraq showed as it withdrew from Kuwait in 1991, and as insurgents have shown in occupied Iraq since 2003.

The success of the oil producing states in taking control of their own oil resources has had important consequences. The massive income from oil has in some places been used to improve the lot of ordinary people, but it has also been used for lavish projects that provide a sense of prestige but little or no practical benefit. Oil income has also given the state a preponderant role in the economy of each country, which has held back the development of the non-oil parts of the economy. For the most part, there has been relatively little diversification and nothing that is at the cutting edge of modern industry, technology or services.

In the Gulf states, oil income has gone into the hands of the ruling families who controlled the state at the point when income surged. Even where the new wealth has been used in part for the general good, it has also helped to ensure the longevity of undemocratic systems of government by allowing ruling elites to defer problems and buy off potential opponents.

The fact that the oil producing states control their oil production means that governments in the world's richest countries must take them seriously. If that were to discourage outside powers from treating the Middle East as a playground for their own interests, it would be to the benefit of the people of the region – but it has not worked out that way.

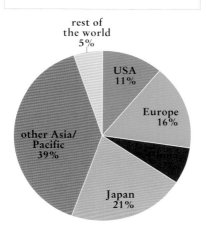

DESTINATION OF MIDDLE EAST EXPORTS
Percentage of total
2006

rest of the world 5%
USA 11%
Europe 16%
China
other Asia/Pacific 39%
Japan 21%

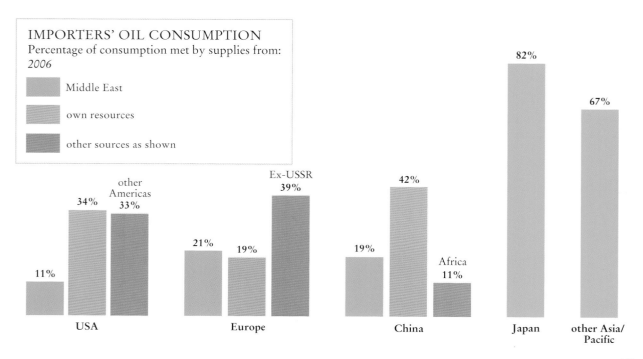

IMPORTERS' OIL CONSUMPTION
Percentage of consumption met by supplies from:
2006

Middle East

own resources

other sources as shown

USA
11%
34%
other Americas 33%

Europe
21%
19%
Ex-USSR 39%

China
19%
42%
Africa 11%

Japan
82%

other Asia/Pacific
67%

THE US PRESENCE

Since 1957, the US presence has been the major influence shaping the Middle East region. Though one of the chief characteristics of US presence and policy, especially from an Arab and Iranian perspective, is its close alignment with Israel, the USA's initial regional interests had little to do with Israel, and were not particularly supportive of Israel's policies. And while many commentators on US policy identify oil as a key, perhaps even *the* key US strategic interest, US policy in the region neither started with oil nor finishes there.

US interest in the Middle East began as an off-shoot of the Cold War as the influence of the old colonial powers waned. The 1956 Suez crisis formed the first watershed in US policy. The USA had been the first government to recognize the newly formed state of Israel in 1948 – and in the lead-up to the foundation of Israel had been supportive in other ways, such as by being willing to fund increased Jewish emigration from Europe to what was then still Mandate Palestine. But in 1956, the USA was firmly against the actions and policy of Britain, France and Israel. The Israeli army defeated Egyptian forces in the Sinai and forced their way to the Suez Canal, but the USA imposed peace and Israeli (as well as British and French) military withdrawal.

US grand strategy during the Cold War was shaped in part by some very traditional notions about power politics, such as the danger of leaving a vacuum, since it would inevitably be filled by the USA's Soviet adversary, which itself developed policies driven by some of the same logic. What was evident in the Suez crisis was that the British and French role in the region was largely played out. The British had dominated Egypt since the 1880s but could neither prevent nor reverse the nationalization of the Suez Canal, and British public and political opinion was deeply divided over the effort to reassert British interests. Its empire was coming to an end – in the region, as elsewhere – and France too, having lost its colonial possessions in South-East Asia, was facing major uprisings for independence in its Arab territories.

The decline of European colonial power was assessed differently in different circles. If Arab nationalists saw the crisis of 1956 as the threshold to independence and the end of an era of humiliation, US strategic analysts saw it as opening the door to Soviet influence in the region. The USSR was comfortable with, and supportive, of the anti-imperialism of the region and was ready to support independence movements and fighters as part of the global struggle against capitalism. Support for newly independent states offered the USSR potential positions of advantage in a global war of manoeuvre. Following its rebuff to Britain, France and Israel, therefore, the USA was concerned to act against rising Soviet influence.

The policy that became known as the Eisenhower Doctrine was set out in March 1957, a few months after the end of the Suez crisis. It included

US REGIONAL MILITARY PRESENCE
November 2007

total US forces

Except in Iraq itself, US military presence in the region has declined since 2005, reflecting Arab governments' anxiety about housing large US forces in the face of popular opposition.

IRAQ

168,000

1,187 US Navy Central Command

BAHRAIN
QATAR

274

512

87

U.A.E.

Gulf of Oman

SAUDI ARABIA

Red Sea

Gulf & Indian Ocean

1 aircraft carrier
1 cruiser
4 destroyers
1 frigate
6 amphibious ships

the undertaking to use armed force to assist any Middle East state that asked for help 'against armed aggression from any country controlled by international communism.' It was essentially an extension of often repeated American policy themes about supporting the opponents of communism everywhere. Because of larger considerations, these new allies were treated by the US administration as friends of freedom on a global level, however little freedom they allowed at home. The Eisenhower Doctrine, like much of American policy throughout the Cold War era, thus looked at regional events through a global lens.

The first action under the Eisenhower Doctrine was a military show of support for King Hussein of Jordan when he was confronted by anti-government riots in 1957. The following year, the Doctrine underpinned a second action involving the direct use of military force, as US marines deployed to Lebanon.

Washington's Doctrines

US policy has from time to time been crystallized in a Doctrine, usually presented in a Presidential speech. The Eisenhower Doctrine in 1957 expressed US concern about Soviet aims and influence in the Middle East. It emphasized economic and military assistance, together with the use of armed force, to resist 'overt armed aggression from any nation controlled by International Communism.' In line with this Doctrine, the USA assisted Jordan's King Hussein in 1957 and sent 10,000 marines to support the Lebanese government in 1958.

In 1969 the Nixon Doctrine revealed less willingness to use force – a response to public dismay at the cost of using American power in Vietnam – and opted for greater reliance on local powers to act as regional 'policemen'.

Following the Soviet invasion of Afghanistan in December 1979, the 1980 Carter Doctrine warned that the USA would use force if its interests in the region were directly threatened by the USSR.

Events in Lebanon in 1958 were the first stage in the unravelling of the constitutional compromise by which the country had gained independence, consisting of a balance of power between the political representatives of the main religious groups in the country. As this fragile arrangement continued to fall apart over the coming years, the country descended into a nightmarish civil war from 1975 to 1990. The events of 1958 were a foretaste of that and resulted from internal causes. Lebanese President Chamoun, however, managed to present the internal political turmoil of 1958 as a matter of Soviet-backed Syrian aggression and the USA intervened by deploying marines in Lebanon for three months.

Perceiving the complex internal politics of Lebanon through a global lens simplified everything. It made action relatively easy to undertake because it was relatively easy to justify. The risks of acting on an over-simple basis, however, could be extreme. As it happened, in 1958, what risks there were produced nothing untoward for US policy or the US marines in Lebanon, largely because the marines stood to one side as a civil war was fought out in which between 2,000 and 4,000 people were killed. In the mid-1980s in Lebanon, the USA again overlooked the complexities of Lebanese and regional politics as it again deployed marines, this time losing well over 200 American lives. And arguably something similar happened another 20 years later as US forces went into Iraq on the basis of a policy that overlooked complex local realities in favour of a global big picture, losing over 2,000 American lives.

Not all US actions, however, have been either military or based on an over-simplified view of the region. In the late 1970s, for example, the Carter administration responded flexibly to the decision by President Sadat of Egypt to ease his country out of the Soviet sphere of influence.

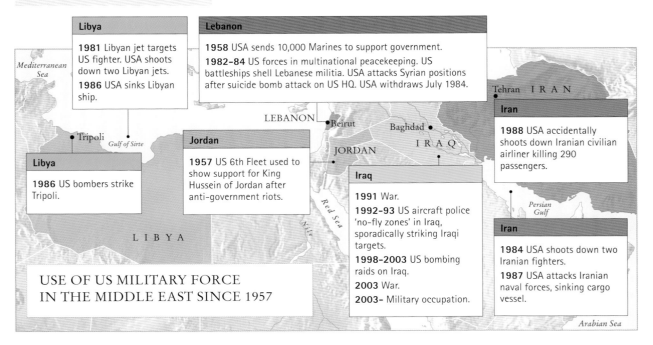

Libya
1981 Libyan jet targets US fighter. USA shoots down two Libyan jets.
1986 USA sinks Libyan ship.

Libya
1986 US bombers strike Tripoli.

Lebanon
1958 USA sends 10,000 Marines to support government.
1982-84 US forces in multinational peacekeeping. US battleships shell Lebanese militia. USA attacks Syrian positions after suicide bomb attack on US HQ. USA withdraws July 1984.

Jordan
1957 US 6th Fleet used to show support for King Hussein of Jordan after anti-government riots.

Iraq
1991 War.
1992-93 US aircraft police 'no-fly zones' in Iraq, sporadically striking Iraqi targets.
1998-2003 US bombing raids on Iraq.
2003 War.
2003- Military occupation.

Iran
1988 USA accidentally shoots down Iranian civilian airliner killing 290 passengers.

Iran
1984 USA shoots down two Iranian fighters.
1987 USA attacks Iranian naval forces, sinking cargo vessel.

USE OF US MILITARY FORCE IN THE MIDDLE EAST SINCE 1957

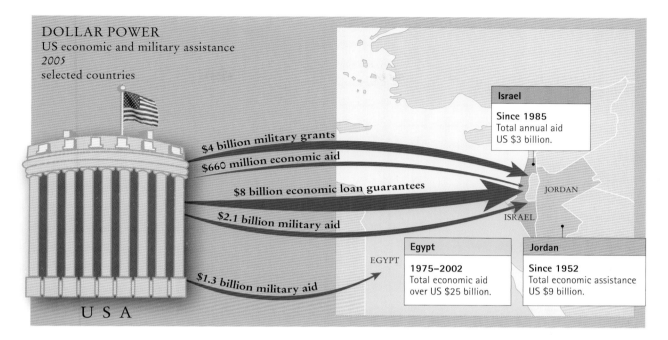

DOLLAR POWER
US economic and military assistance
2005
selected countries

$4 billion military grants

$660 million economic aid

$8 billion economic loan guarantees

$2.1 billion military aid

$1.3 billion military aid

U S A

Israel
Since 1985
Total annual aid
US $3 billion.

JORDAN

ISRAEL

EGYPT

Egypt
1975–2002
Total economic aid
over US $25 billion.

Jordan
Since 1952
Total economic assistance
US $9 billion.

US diplomatic assistance and the promise of much increased economic support was crucial in achieving the 1979 agreement by which Israel returned Sinai to Egyptian control.

By this time, in a development that gathered momentum with the 1967 Arab-Israeli war and was confirmed by the 1973 war, the USA had become Israel's biggest arms supplier and its aid and cheap loans were a major component of Israel's economic viability. At the same time, successive US administrations were careful not to let Israel be their only regional ally. The Nixon Doctrine in 1969 attempted to move US policy away from the commitment to act with armed force and therefore stressed the role of local powers in the Middle East as elsewhere. It was partly to ensure unity and cooperation against Soviet-backed threats that the USA promoted peaceful solutions to Arab-Israeli issues, in an effort to take the heat out of Arab-Israeli relations.

Beyond the policies and actions of the USA, there is another dimension to US influence, which is to be found at a more general, popular-cultural level, in Hollywood movies, international electronic news media and the internet. Many of the styles of consumerism – including, not least, women's dress – and ways of thinking that are projected as an integral part of cultural production worldwide offer direct challenges to Muslim traditions, as they do to all sorts of tradition everywhere. The homogenizing force of modernity is a challenge and affront in a multitude of places, and it is widely discussed as such, opposed and directly resisted. In many places, and not the Middle East alone, modernity is perceived as essentially American. And in the Middle East, many commentators perceive the political and the cultural dimensions as one and the same.

PART TWO ARENAS OF CONFLICT

Since World War II ended in 1945, the Middle East has experienced only one year in which there was no armed conflict going on — 1947. With that exception, there has been continual warfare, though not everywhere in the region. In the experience of war, as in many other ways, the region shows considerable internal diversity.

Compared to elsewhere in the world, however, the Middle East does not stand out as unique in the frequency and pervasiveness of war. Nor are its wars outstandingly lethal compared to other regions. The wars with the highest death tolls in the region so far have been the Algerian war of independence of 1956 to 1962 and the Iran-Iraq war of 1980 to 1988; in sub-Saharan Africa and several regions of Asia, there have been several wars with equal or greater death tolls.

Where the Middle East does stand out is in the global significance of its wars. They brought the superpowers to the brink of nuclear confrontation during the Cold War. Some of them directly affect the economic well-being of rich and poor countries alike because of oil — sometimes because oil is used as a diplomatic weapon, and sometimes because war drives its price up. They contain an inbuilt risk of escalation and spillover, not only because the conflict issues go so deep but also because of the involvement of outside powers. Parties to some of the wars have not hesitated to export the violence to different parts of Europe, and it is in the name of conflicts in the region that al-Qaida and groups inspired by it have brought large scale terrorism to the USA and Europe in the 21st century.

In modern armed conflict, the frontline of suffering always involves civilians — killed or wounded by bombs dropped from the sky or detonated in cars and buses, by rockets and artillery, by snipers; driven forcibly from their homes or running for their lives; grieving for family members killed in action; caring for those disabled and traumatized by violence. It is questionable whether this concern features at all prominently in the strategic thinking of more than a handful of those who give the orders in more than a handful of conflicts. The suffering of ordinary people, after all, has proven to be itself a weapon with which political leaders attempt to impose their will.

Aftermath of war,
Beirut, 1992

ARAB-ISRAELI WARFARE

Israel was founded amid war and violence, which continued throughout the 1950s in the form of guerrilla raids by Palestinians, Israeli counter-strikes and reprisals, and was punctuated by war against Egypt in 1956. The pattern continued into the 1960s and culminated in a period of virtually permanent warfare from 1967 to 1973. The end of the 1973 war marked the end of one strategic era in the region and ushered in a new one, in which, though the dangers for people living there were just as acute, the nature and the source of the dangers changed.

In February 1966, Ba'athists took power in Syria and attacks on Israeli border areas intensified. Israel was never slow to retaliate. In November, in the name of Arab solidarity, President Nasser of Egypt was virtually duty-bound to accept a Syrian request for a comprehensive defence agreement between the two states. For Nasser, the trouble was that Egypt's policy was then hitched to Syria's. As the acknowledged leader of the non-monarchical Arab states, he was forced into a position where he was leading from behind.

In May 1967 Nasser started to lead from the front, with a dramatic political and military escalation that included blockading Israel's access to the Red Sea through the Straits of Tiran. He also asked UN forces to leave the Gaza strip, where they had been stationed since the 1956 Suez War, and moved Egyptian forces across the Canal into Sinai. Rhetoric escalated at the same time and at the end of the month other Arab states moved forces close to Israel's borders

It was clear that war was imminent. It was no surprise if Israel were to strike first and hard; the new state had never been reluctant to assert itself militarily, striking against West Bank Palestinian villages from which guerrilla attacks originated. One famous operation in Qibya in 1953 killed 69 Palestinian villagers in retaliation for the murder of an Israeli woman and her two children. Even against that background, the comprehensive nature of Israel's opening strike on 5 June was a shock. In a single day, Israel attacked Egypt's 17 airfields and destroyed most of its air force, following up with a rapid army offensive in Sinai that reached the Suez Canal four days later. At the same time, Israeli forces occupied the Old City of Jerusalem and took control of the West Bank, and then attacked Syrian forces in the Golan Heights.

Israel was determined to hold onto the newly occupied territory. The UN Security Council passed Resolution 242 calling on Israel to withdraw from territories occupied in the war; Israel and its supporters have ever since insisted on interpreting this as meaning some territories, not all. With the additional territory, Israel expected better security. It was also not a small gain that, with the conquest of the West Bank, Israel took control of the area's underground water sources, with which to make up for the shortfall in its own supplies resulting from its heavy use of water for irrigation.

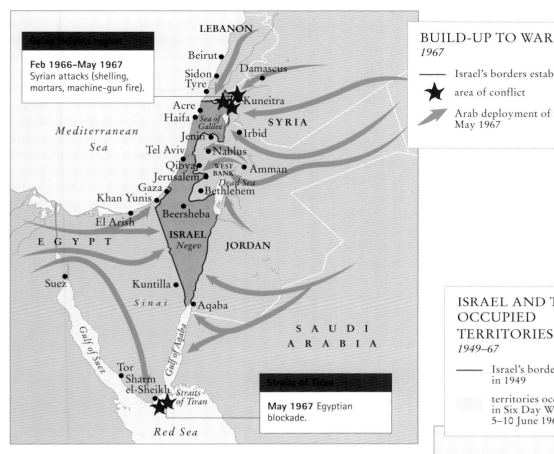

BUILD-UP TO WAR
1967

—— Israel's borders established in 1949

★ area of conflict

➤ Arab deployment of forces May 1967

Golar Heights region

Feb 1966–May 1967
Syrian attacks (shelling, mortars, machine-gun fire).

Straits of Tiran

May 1967 Egyptian blockade.

ISRAEL AND THE OCCUPIED TERRITORIES
1949–67

—— Israel's borders established in 1949

territories occupied by Israel in Six Day War, 5–10 June 1967

From an Arab perspective, the 1967 war was an unmitigated disaster. It showed once again that Arab agreement on the objective of defeating Israel did not translate into practical unity; as in 1948, there was no unified system of military command and Israel's military superiority was visibly overwhelming. The war resulted in loss of territory by three states, with 200,000 Palestinian refugees crossing the Jordan River, and the 600,000 Palestinians who stayed in the West Bank coming under Israeli military control.

The 1967 war marked the end – or at least the beginning of the end – of Egypt's Arab leadership and above all led not only to a pervasive feeling of bitterness and powerlessness but also, motivated by that, a search for, explanations. Some Arab writers argued that Israel's military superiority and political unity and firmness of purpose derived from it being a state founded on religion, and began to argue for the Arab world to follow suit and restore its own basis in faith.

Between the 1967 and 1973 wars, the Middle East became an arena of Cold War conflict, with the USA strongly backing Israel and the USSR supporting its major adversaries. In both cases, support took political, economic and military forms.

Diplomatic initiatives came and went but nothing changed. The lack of movement deepened Arab and Palestinian frustration and resentment, while suiting the Israeli side rather well. Meanwhile violent conflict continued. There was the familiar pattern of guerrilla raids on Israeli targets and counter-strikes, plus artillery bombardments, bombing strikes and occasional commando raids along the Suez Canal in what was known as the War of Attrition from 1969 to 1970. The label is revealingly inaccurate, for attrition is a process by which one side, or both, is steadily if slowly worn down, whereas this was at most an irritant for Israel and for Egypt an empty gesture – an attempt to show that, despite crushing defeat in 1967, it continued to fight for the Arab cause.

Leadership of the PLO changed with the election of the dynamic Yasser Arafat as Chairman. Defeated in orthodox war, Arab states were prepared to finance the PLO's build-up. Based in Jordan, its prestige grew and it mounted joint operations with the Jordanian army against Israeli forces. But factions in the Jordanian army saw the PLO's growth and the size of the Palestinian refugee population as threats to Jordan's stability. In September 1970, mounting tensions boiled over into a one-week civil war that ended with the expulsion of the PLO from Jordan.

Neither orthodox war nor guerrilla attacks could overthrow or even weaken Israel, which led some Palestinian groups to turn to terrorism; there were hijackings of commercial aircraft and attacks such as at the Munich Olympics in 1972 when 11 Israeli hostages were murdered by the Black September group.

Against this backdrop, Anwar Sadat, Egypt's new President from 1970, wanted to change the diplomatic landscape and make new initiatives possible. He wanted to free Egypt's development prospects from the burden of confrontation with Israel. Though his 1972 request to the USSR to withdraw its military advisers seemed to reflect his long-term goal of peace, his next move was for war.

Attacking on Yom Kippur, the Day of Atonement in the Jewish religious calendar, Egyptian and Syrian forces gained the advantage of surprise and for once cooperated closely. Egyptian forces struck deep into Sinai. The political unity of the Arab states was also striking; they successfully used their control of oil to gain concessions from western Europe and Japan. Within this unity, however, disunity persisted. Egypt and Syria had very different aims; Syria wanted to regain territory lost in 1967, while Egypt wanted to get diplomacy moving.

In the war, Israel regained the initiative and its forces crossed the Suez and, in the north, entered Syria. The superpowers made enormous emergency arms transfers to their respective allies. When a US-brokered and UN-approved cease-fire was not fully implemented on time, the USSR announced it was considering unilaterally deploying forces to the region. The USA responded with a worldwide military and nuclear alert.

The 1973 war was neither triumph nor cataclysm. Israel prevailed but no longer looked invulnerable. In both human and economic terms, the 1973 war was the most expensive of Israel's wars so far. Its death toll of

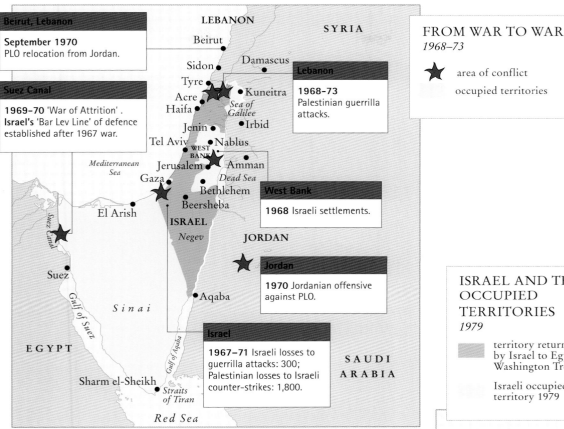

Beirut, Lebanon

September 1970
PLO relocation from Jordan.

Suez Canal

1969–70 'War of Attrition'.
Israel's 'Bar Lev Line' of defence
established after 1967 war.

FROM WAR TO WAR
1968–73

★ area of conflict

  occupied territories

Lebanon

1968–73
Palestinian guerrilla
attacks.

West Bank

1968 Israeli settlements.

Jordan

1970 Jordanian offensive
against PLO.

Israel

1967–71 Israeli losses to
guerrilla attacks: 300;
Palestinian losses to Israeli
counter-strikes: 1,800.

2,500 was more than three times as high as in 1967. And despite all the USA's help, the war cost Israel the equivalent of one full year's economic output. Within Israel, the government was blamed for complacency, lack of readiness, and a confused and uncertain response when the Egyptian offensive began. As a result, Labour, which was the largest party in the government and had been in every Israeli government since independence, began to lose ground. In the 1977 election, its vote – normally around 40 percent – fell to 25 percent and the Likud opposition came to power for the first time.

Sadat finally achieved the diplomatic renewal he sought by flying dramatically to Israel in 1977 to address the Knesset (parliament). Negotiations the following year produced the Washington Treaty of 1979 under which Israel withdrew from the Sinai. Sadat was abused and isolated by the other Arab states, and his initiative brought to a close the first era of Israeli-Arab relations. Thenceforth, the major sources of insecurity for Israel were not to come from Arab states but from Palestinian guerrillas. By then a new factor had entered the equation: from the mid-1970s, Israel was counted as a nuclear armed state, though for a further decade it would neither confirm nor deny the fact.

ISRAEL AND THE OCCUPIED TERRITORIES
1979

  territory returned
  by Israel to Egypt in 1979
  Washington Treaty

  Israeli occupied
  territory 1979

ISRAEL AND PALESTINE

The issues in the Israel-Palestine conflict come down to a question of land – who can live there and who controls its use. This has been overlaid with issues of human rights and international law, coloured by mutual bitterness and mistrust after decades of violence. Every fact, every statistic, every argument and every legal interpretation of every resolution, judgement and document is contested. What is incontestable is that both sides have used frightening violence against the other, and that ordinary citizens as well as fighters have suffered.

The Israeli settlement in the West Bank started in 1968. By the start of the 21st century there were 400,000 Israelis living in Gaza and the West Bank including east Jerusalem. What were called settlements were in many cases well-established small towns. All are illegal under the Fourth Geneva Convention of 1949 – part of what was formerly called the Law of War and is now known as International Humanitarian Law. The Fourth Convention bans a state from moving civilian population into occupied territory. Everything that is done to that end is also illegal, including anything done to perpetuate the situation. This was the basis of

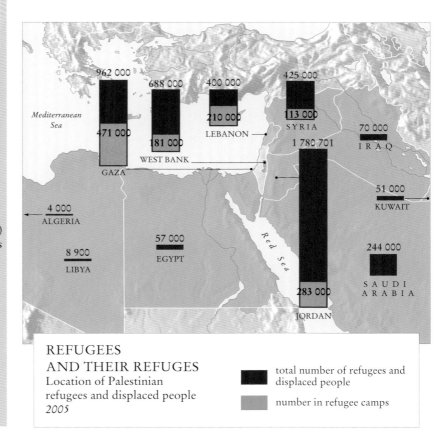

REFUGEES AND THEIR REFUGES
Location of Palestinian refugees and displaced people
2005

■ total number of refugees and displaced people

■ number in refugee camps

56

the International Court of Justice ruling in 2004 that the wall being built as a security barrier between Israel and the West Bank is illegal, because parts of its route link settlements to the main territory of Israel.

In 1988, the Palestine National Council – the law-making body for the Palestine Liberation Organization – was persuaded by its leader Yasser Arafat to recognize Israel within its 1949 boundaries. This entailed accepting that Palestinians had no claim to govern 78 percent of historic Palestine. For the PLO, its struggle thereafter centred on the West Bank and Gaza, but Israelis were entitled to question the firmness of the change in position for no action was taken to amend the Palestine National Charter accordingly. The Islamic Resistance Movement, Hamas, had not recognized Israel as a legal state by the time it formed the government of the Palestine Authority (PA) in 2006. However, most observers believed that it would have to do so in some way, even if it eventually uses a form of words that distinguishes what is legal from what it believes is legitimate.

The issue for Palestinians is not simply the presence of settlers in the West Bank and – until 2005 – in Gaza. It is Israeli control of the territory, its use of water resources, the constraints it places on Palestinians' economic prospects, the way Israeli forces treat Palestinians. It is also, therefore, an issue of dignity and hope being permanently under attack, both as a community and as individuals. Out of this comes the urge to fight back and take the war to the Israeli civilians. And, characteristically for persistent conflict, the measures Israel takes to blunt the threat of violence serve to exacerbate the underlying problem, even when they have some impact in enhancing Israel's short-term security.

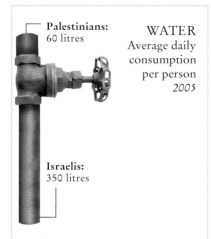

Palestinians: 60 litres

Israelis: 350 litres

WATER
Average daily consumption per person
2005

Upon occupying the West Bank in 1967 Israel declared all water resources to be its property and instituted a strict system of licensing the construction of new wells and pipes. Since 1982, increased Israeli use has dried up Palestinian wells. Israel is slow to approve new water projects for Palestinian use, controls how much water can be used by Palestinians and does not hide the fact that more water goes to the Jewish settlements in the Occupied Territories than to the ordinary Palestinian residents.

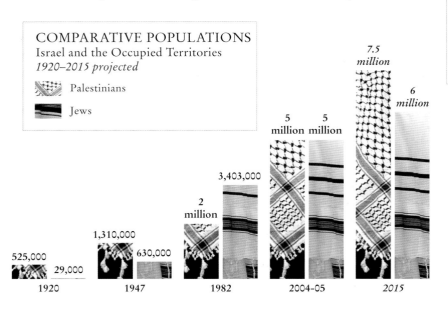

COMPARATIVE POPULATIONS
Israel and the Occupied Territories
1920–2015 projected

Palestinians

Jews

				7.5 million
			5 million / 5 million	6 million
		3,403,000		
	2 million			
525,000 / 29,000	1,310,000 / 630,000			
1920	1947	1982	2004-05	*2015*

INTIFADA AND POLITICS

The first *intifada* was a people's movement that pitted stone-throwing youths against Israeli armed forces. The images it generated won international sympathy. Israel's standing had been diminished by intervention in Lebanon in 1982 and it now faced the risk of international isolation. The US administration pushed it into the Madrid Peace Conference in 1991, but the conference quickly got bogged down. A quiet Norwegian initiative in 1993 was more productive. Israel wanted a way out of the *intifada*, while the PLO wanted to get back to Palestine from its Tunisian exile. An agreement was initialled in Oslo and formally signed at the White House to set up a phased peace process, gradually giving Palestinians more autonomy.

The *intifada* ended and the PLO came home but there was no real peace. The Oslo agreement deferred the difficult issues, on the theory that agreeing straightforward issues would make it easier to agree the difficult issues later. It was not a bad theory but, in this case, it did not work. Militants on both sides saw too much concession and too little gain. The settlements were not closed, and from 1996 started to expand

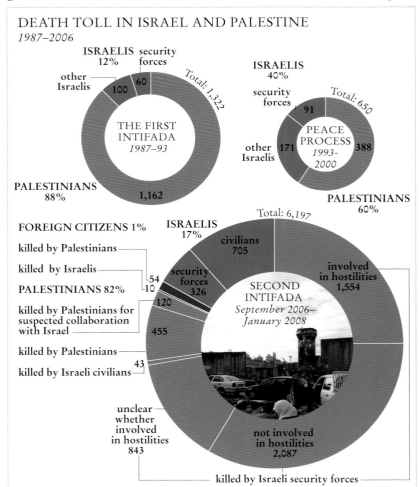

DEATH TOLL IN ISRAEL AND PALESTINE
1987–2006

THE FIRST INTIFADA *1987–93*
Total: 1,322
ISRAELIS 12%
security forces 60
other Israelis 100
PALESTINIANS 88% 1,162

PEACE PROCESS *1993-2000*
Total: 650
ISRAELIS 40%
security forces 91
other Israelis 171
388
PALESTINIANS 60%

SECOND INTIFADA *September 2006– January 2008*
Total: 6,197
FOREIGN CITIZENS 1%
killed by Palestinians 54
killed by Israelis 10
PALESTINIANS 82%
killed by Palestinians for suspected collaboration with Israel 120
killed by Palestinians 455
killed by Israeli civilians 43
unclear whether involved in hostilities 843
ISRAELIS 17%
civilians 705
security forces 326
involved in hostilities 1,554
not involved in hostilities 2,087
killed by Israeli security forces

again, and there were insecurity and killings on both sides; indeed, more Israelis died in six years after Oslo than before it. Four more years of talks achieved intermittent progress towards agreement, but the gains were always insecure, though the level of violence subsided in 1998–99.

The second *intifada* was triggered by Likud party leader Ariel Sharon's visit to the area known to Israelis as Temple Mount and to Palestinians as Haram al-Sharif – the site of the al-Aqsa mosque. Sharon was a distinguished soldier, former defence minister, a security hard-liner, and a forthright supporter of the settlements. Whether the motive for the visit was provocative or innocent, the result was an explosion of protest. Initially, the second *intifada* was like the first, but escalated as Islamic Jihad, Hamas and the al-Aqsa Martyrs Brigade mobilized suicide bombers. In response, Israel reoccupied parts of the West Bank, placing Yasser Arafat's headquarters in Ramallah under siege. Both sides took the war to the civilians on the other side and each side justified itself by the actions of the other. Palestinian militants' actions were more deadly than in the first *intifada* and there was less international sympathy for the Palestinians.

During the Oslo years, the PA had little chance to establish good governance in the West Bank and Gaza; much of its income came as international assistance via Israel, whose security forces were omnipresent, even when things were peaceful. But what little chance the PA had, it wasted through nepotism, corruption, incompetence and abuse of human rights.

Disillusion with the PA led to support for Hamas, founded in 1988 out of a social welfare movement that originally started as an offshoot from the Muslim Brotherhood. Where the PA seemed weak against Israel, incompetent and corrupt, Hamas looked strong, competent and clean. Arafat's death in 2004 released Palestinian public opinion from its loyalty to his movement; in January 2006 Hamas beat al-Fatah and won the PA elections. The USA and European governments, having long insisted that the Palestinian leadership be elected, decided the Palestinian people had made the wrong choice and refused to deal with Hamas. Even a coalition government of Hamas and al-Fatah in 2006-07 proved unacceptable. In 2007 Hamas and al-Fatah fought openly and Hamas took control of Gaza through force of arms.

Israel is also politically divided. The 1993 agreement with the PLO was the topic of bitter controversy. Electoral fortunes swung between Likud and Labour. As the second *intifada* wore on, many Israelis no longer saw the settlers as heroes, but rather as part of Israel's problem. Recognition that there would have to be some withdrawal from the Occupied Territories grew, even among their strongest supporters, including Sharon. To take the option up, he had to quit Likud and form a new party, Kadima ('Forward'). Though successive strokes left Sharon in a coma, his party came out in front in the March 2006 election. Its task then was to put together a coalition government to implement the option of limited withdrawal.

PALESTINIAN ELECTIONS
January 2006
Turnout: 77 percent

Fatah 43 seats — Hamas 76 seats

PFLP 3 seats — Badeel 2 seats — Independent Palestine 2 seats — Third Way 2 seats

ISRAELI ELECTIONS
March 2006
Turnout: 62 percent

Torah Judaism 6 seats — Shas 12 seats

Kadima 29 seats — Labour 20 seats — Likud 12 seats

National Union Religious Party 9 seats — Pensioners 7 seats — Yisrael Beitenu 11 seats — Meretz 5 seats — Arab parties 9 seats

PEACE PLAN

As Prime Minister, Sharon decided the PLO was not a worthwhile counterpart for negotiations and decided to impose a peace plan unilaterally. Announced in 2004, it involved withdrawing all settlements from Gaza and some from the West Bank. Despite settlers' resistance, the Gaza withdrawal was accomplished in 2005. From a Palestinian perspective, the gains were not real: Israel gave up 19 square miles and took 23 square miles in the same period; 8,500 settlers left Gaza in 2005 and 14,000 moved into the West Bank

Imposing a peace settlement is a tricky idea, realistic only if the side that is dissatisfied has absolutely no option for fighting back. Israel's military power is overwhelming compared to the PA and all the Palestinian armed groups combined. And the wall being built as a security barrier is intended not just to mark a boundary but to be a defence against infiltration. Whether this is enough to stop suicide bombers getting through to civilian targets in Israel, however, is far from certain.

Important components of the plan remained unclear and in flux long after construction of the wall began. Official Israeli information revealed that the Palestinians would be caught between the wall and the Jordan Valley, with Palestinian land divided into three chunks – one area north of Nablus and Tulkarm, from which Israeli forces would withdraw, a second between Nablus and Jerusalem, and a third to the south of Jerusalem –

ISRAEL

Army: **133,000** plus **500,000** ready reserves,
Airforce: **34,000** plus **55,000** reserves,
Navy: **9,500** plus **10,000** ready reserves

1,176 field artillery

3,501 battle tanks

10,419 armoured personnel carriers

393 combat aircraft

94 attack helicopters

100+ surface-to-surface missiles (including nuclear capable)

224 multiple rocket launchers

PALESTINE AUTHORITY

56,000 paramilitary including **9,000** police plus presidential security, civil defence, intelligence services

Armed groups — estimated **2,000** in Fatah-connected groups
500 in Hamas
some **2,500** other

BALANCE OF POWER
Israeli and Palestinian armed forces
2008

surface-to-surface missiles: some in the hands of armed groups plus the area round Jericho. Each chunk is to be criss-crossed by Israeli roads that will primarily be for settlers and the military. Walls along some of these roads would make them impossible to cross except at checkpoints. No farming, building or other development is permitted near the roads. The route of the wall brings many settlements – including areas where settlement building is planned but not yet done – into direct contact with Israel proper, in the process slicing up Palestinian farming areas and taking over more West Bank land including areas where Palestinians live.

Israel justifies this through the needs of security, but the consequence is to make daily life harder for Palestinians, making commerce more difficult and leading to the collapse of the economy during 2006–07. If there is to be a Palestinian state on the West Bank, it will not be geographically unified and could not be governed efficiently. Israel's policies thus continue to feed resentment and desperation among Palestinians and the urge to strike back.

Israel does not accept Hamas as a legitimate voice of the Palestinians and is supported in this by the USA and European governments. But it is not clear the al-Fatah movement, were it to make an agreement with Israel, could do so with majority Palestinian support. And if Hamas does not live up to Palestinian expectations a more radical and militant alternative may emerge, outflanking Hamas just as it once outflanked the PLO.

ISRAEL'S PLANS FOR THE WEST BANK AND GAZA
2007

—— Israel/West Bank 1949 boundary

—— Israeli Wall, or 'Security Fence', dividing Israel from the West Bank

—— Israeli settlement access roads actual, projected or under construction

● Israeli controlled major crossing point

☐ West Bank land cut off by the wall

Projected areas of control

Palestine Authority

Israeli

Israel

Exact details of Israel's plans for the West Bank and the security barrier have not been made clear and the plan has changed from time to time, but enough official information is available for the broad shape to be clear.

61

LEBANON

For Lebanon to be peaceful, its government and political class would have to achieve two things: transcend politics based on religious difference, and steer the country away from the dangers posed by its geographic location next to Syria and Israel. While Lebanon has been independent, no political leader able to do that has emerged. Most of the time, Lebanese politics have been characterized by the opposite; rivalries between the different faith groups, and tactical alliances with one neighbour or the other. Lebanon's tragedy in the 1970s and 1980s was in part a spin-off from the Israel-Palestine conflict.

At the same time as these violent and complex political rivalries and manoeuvres made victims out of Lebanese citizens, they were also a trap for outside powers. Israel, Syria, the USA, Italy and France all intervened, only to get caught up in factional politics, shifting alliances and in-fighting. All five eventually withdrew under pressure and in some disarray.

Lebanon's diverse population includes Shi'a and Sunni Muslims, the two main Islamic groups worldwide, as well as Druze, and Christians of various denominations, among which the largest group are the Maronites. Whether the Druze have ethnic origins distinct from other groups in Lebanon is open to argument; an off-shoot from the dissident Ismaeli branch of Shi'ism, Druze have existed for at least a millennium. The Maronites' history, of which the details and origins are also contestable, goes back to a schism in the Byzantine Church in the first millennium CE. Both the Druze and the Maronites faced and rejected pressures to conform and produced a martial tradition of self-defence and resistance, which in the 19th and 20th centuries led to the organization of militias. As the Ottoman Empire weakened in the 19th century, tensions and rivalries between Druze and Maronites led to violence. From about 1860, a key aim of French policy was to support the Maronites.

As in other parts of the Ottoman Empire, identity became the basis of politics and power; in this case, religious identity. When France received the League of Nations' Mandate for Lebanon after World War I, it promoted a constitution based on religious affiliation that favoured the Maronites. After World War II, when France was forced by local resistance, supported by British pressure, to relinquish Lebanon and Syria (leaving with an artillery bombardment of Damascus that killed 500 civilians), sectarian rivalry was hard-wired into the newly independent state of Lebanon.

This rivalry was moderated by the 1943 National Pact. Under it, the Maronites accepted an Arab identity for the new state, which joined the Arab League as a founder member; for their part, Muslim political groups accepted Lebanon's borders and a disadvantageous share-out of parliamentary seats based on the 1932 census.

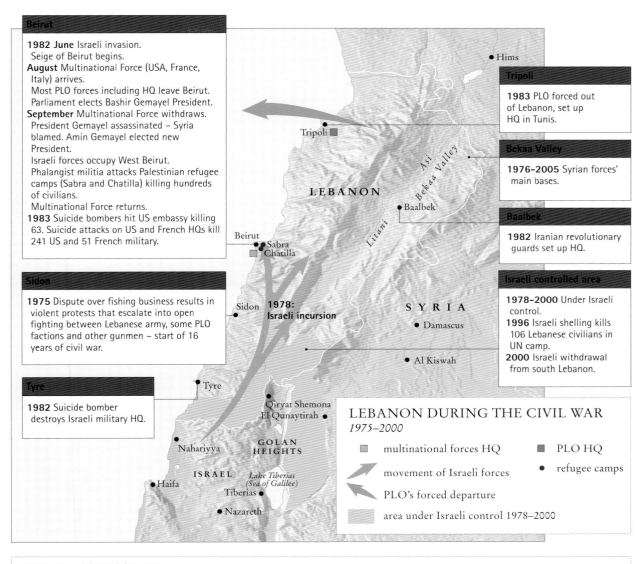

Beirut

1982 June Israeli invasion.
Seige of Beirut begins.
August Multinational Force (USA, France, Italy) arrives.
Most PLO forces including HQ leave Beirut.
Parliament elects Bashir Gemayel President.
September Multinational Force withdraws.
President Gemayel assassinated – Syria blamed. Amin Gemayel elected new President.
Israeli forces occupy West Beirut.
Phalangist militia attacks Palestinian refugee camps (Sabra and Chatilla) killing hundreds of civilians.
Multinational Force returns.
1983 Suicide bombers hit US embassy killing 63. Suicide attacks on US and French HQs kill 241 US and 51 French military.

Tripoli

1983 PLO forced out of Lebanon, set up HQ in Tunis.

Bekaa Valley

1976–2005 Syrian forces' main bases.

Baalbek

1982 Iranian revolutionary guards set up HQ.

Sidon

1975 Dispute over fishing business results in violent protests that escalate into open fighting between Lebanese army, some PLO factions and other gunmen – start of 16 years of civil war.

Israeli controlled area

1978–2000 Under Israeli control.
1996 Israeli shelling kills 106 Lebanese civilians in UN camp.
2000 Israeli withdrawal from south Lebanon.

Tyre

1982 Suicide bomber destroys Israeli military HQ.

LEBANON DURING THE CIVIL WAR
1975–2000

▪ multinational forces HQ   ▪ PLO HQ

→ movement of Israeli forces   • refugee camps

→ PLO's forced departure

▨ area under Israeli control 1978–2000

THE PARTIES TO WAR
1982–84

Palestine
• PLO
• Popular Front for the Liberation of Palestine – General Command
• Abu Musa faction
• Palestinian Liberation Army
Iran
• Iranian Revolutionary Guards

Lebanon
• Government
• Christian forces: Phalange militia (dominant in the Lebanese forces); Republic of Southern Lebanon
• Muslim forces: Druze militia; Shi'a groups – Hizbollah, Amal, Jundallah (Soldiers of God), Huseyn Suicide Commandos, the Dawah (Call) Party

Israel
Syria
Multinational Force
• USA
• France
• Italy
Other
• Syrian Social Nationalist Party
• Lebanese Communist Party
• al-Saiqa

CIVIL WAR

By the 1960s most Muslims and many observers believed demographic shifts meant the Maronites were now in a minority. The unity and pragmatism inspired by imminent independence in the 1940s were long gone.

The basic fault lines of ethnic politics were exacerbated by the weakness of the Lebanese state. In the hands of competing Maronite groups, the state was an instrument for their own power. There was a murderous rivalry between Maronite political parties and their militias. The state could not rise above this conflict and arbitrate because it was neither detached enough nor strong enough. When war began in 1975, the Lebanese Army was outnumbered about two to one by its opponents.

A further problem lay in the Palestine issue. When Israel was founded, 120,000 Palestinian refugees fled to Lebanon; more followed after the 1967 war. Southern Lebanon was a launching ground for attacks on northern Israel and was, therefore, always at risk of reprisal raids. In 1970, when the PLO was forced out of Jordan it moved its headquarters to Beirut. It grew in strength and international prestige but many Lebanese saw its fighters as armed, arrogant intruders. As Jordanian army officers had feared would happen in their own country, the PLO became something of a parallel government – pursuing its own interests, which meant fighting Israel, not maintaining Lebanon as a peaceful, stable country.

The explosion came with a dispute about business deals in Sidon's fishing industry. The fighting quickly escalated, drew in all the armed groups, and killed 50,000 people by the time it subsided in early 1976 as a result of Syrian military intervention. Syrian President Assad distrusted PLO leader Yasser Arafat and believed the PLO was becoming too powerful. He aimed not just to end the fighting but to strengthen the Maronites and weaken the PLO who, together with its left-wing Druze allies, controlled about 80 percent of the country at that point.

The Syrian intervention temporarily subdued some of the violence but the war did not end. Israel sent in forces to southern Lebanon in 1978 and north to Beirut in 1982. Fighting escalated until the Multinational Force (MNF) arrived and oversaw the departure of the PLO, which had been badly weakened both by Israeli forces and by a Syrian-backed internal mutiny. The MNF withdrew after only a few weeks, and returned after a few more weeks following the massacres of Palestinians in the Sabra and Chatilla refugee camps. These were carried out by Maronite Phalangist militias in an area controlled by the Israeli army. The period immediately after the MNF's return offered promises of reconstruction and order, which came to nothing. New forces were rising in the country to try to drive the Israelis out, especially Shi'a forces. The Amal militia had formed in 1975; some of its members trained Iran's Revolutionary Guards, who in turn sponsored and trained Hizbollah, formed in 1982. As the 1980s wore on, Hizbollah and Amal entered a violent rivalry. The MNF's will was already wilting by the time suicide bombers detonated massive bombs in simultaneous attacks on American and French headquarters in 1983.

The MNF's departure was followed by a further six years of mayhem, characterized by brutal fighting, and kidnapping of some of the few foreigners who remained – diplomats and journalists. There were further attacks on Palestinian refugees – this time by Muslim militia – and the conditions of life for ordinary people worsened as the Lebanese state disintegrated. By 1988 there were two Prime Ministers – put differently, there was no legitimate Prime Minister – and the Maronite Christian forces entered a final phase of internecine warfare that weakened all factions to the point that Syria could push through the Taif Accord. This offered peace through constitutional change and Syrian military occupation and political control.

Israel remained in control of a zone in southern Lebanon. Its complicity in the Sabra and Chatilla massacres shocked and alienated much international public opinion and many Israelis and tarnished then Defence Minister Ariel Sharon. He resigned and was later named by an Israeli official enquiry as partially responsible along with other politicians, officials and officers. The occupation of southern Lebanon continued to be controversial. And still the depth and extent of Shi'a resistance ensured there were no clear security gains for Israel. It finally pulled out in 2000, not exactly defeated by its 22-year intervention in Lebanon, but not successful either.

Syria was left as the dominant outside power, its position secured by the Taif Accord. But many Lebanese came to resent its role and the presence of a million Syrian workers during the reconstruction period. A manoeuvre in 2004 to keep the President in power backfired as Lebanese politicians succeeded in getting the UN to urge Syria to pull out of Lebanon. When the architect of this diplomatic success, ex-PM Rafiq Hariri, was killed by a car bomb, Syria was universally accused despite its protestations of innocence. Whether the murder was a government decision or the work of a secret service faction, the political fall-out was quick and Syrian forces left within months of Hariri's death. Attitudes to that event remain key markers of political allegiance in Lebanon.

Two further blows shook the country's peaceful development in 2006 and 2007. First, when Hizbollah took two Israeli soldiers prisoner, the Israeli response was more forceful than expected. Yet Israel was equally surprised by the strength of Hizbollah's resistance in southern Lebanon and its capacity for missile strikes on Israel during the one-month war. Over 1,100 Lebanese civilians died, as well as a disputed number of Hizbollah fighters (estimates range from 64 to 700), 46 army personnel and 17 Amal fighters. For Israel, about 120 soldiers and 44 civilians died.

In November 2007, President Lahoud's extended term of office ended with Lebanon's divided politicians unable to agree on a successor. Crisis escalated and persisted against a background of continuing political assassinations and the killing of seven people at a demonstration against power cuts in January 2008. Who was responsible was unknown. After six decades of independence, the combined challenge of confessional politics and regional insecurity still looked insuperable.

The Constitution and the Taif Accord

Lebanon's constitution was adopted at French behest in 1926 when the country was administered by France under the League of Nations' Mandate. It divided power according to religious affiliation, with the balance of advantage for the Maronite Christians, France's particular allies. The President was always to be a Christian, the Prime Minister (appointed by the President) a Sunni Muslim, and the Speaker of the Parliament a Shi'ite. When Lebanon gained independence in 1943, an unwritten National Pact used the 1932 population census to assign parliamentary seats in a six to five ratio in favour of the Christians. There was no mechanism in the constitution to change the ratio if the population balance changed, as it was widely believed to have done by the 1960s. Though the constitution was amended in other ways, the religious balance was left unchanged.

In 1989, in an effort to end the war, a meeting of Lebanon's MPs in Taif, Saudi Arabia, agreed constitutional amendments that marginally weakened the Maronite grip on power by having the Prime Minister appointed by Parliament, while both Parliament and Cabinet were to divide seats equally between Christians and Muslims. The Taif Accord left the faith-based core of the constitution intact and also conceded to Syria a direct role in Lebanese government.

SYRIA

The difficulties that Western governments and commentators have in interpreting Syria's distinctive foreign policy mixture of militancy and pragmatism are encapsulated by the paradox that Syria is the only state that simultaneously features on the official US list of state sponsors of terrorism, while having formal diplomatic relations with the USA and actively cooperating with the USA in counter-terrorism.

The current president, Bashar al-Assad, like his late father and predecessor, Hafez al-Assad, is an Alawi. This religious group makes up about 12 percent of Syria's population. Alawi origins are pre-Islamic and the group appears to have absorbed and interpreted the fundamentals of Islam in its own distinctive way; details are not known because of traditional Alawi secrecy about their religion. A weak and impoverished minority for centuries, the community benefited after independence from the rise to prominence of a significant number of Alawis. There was something of a backlash against this in the mid-1960s, but Hafez al-Assad's assumption of the presidency in 1970 opened the door for many more Alawis to take key positions. To a significant degree, though not exclusively, the government's power is buttressed by Alawi loyalties.

In 1973 the issue of religion and power came out into the open with demands from some groups that Islam be declared the state religion, an especially pointed demand since many Sunni Muslims refuse to acknowledge that the Alawi faith is in fact Islamic. A resurgence of violence in the late 1970s culminated in a major uprising and open fighting in the city of Hama in 1982; reliable sources indicate that 10,000 or more civilians were killed by the Syrian army.

It is in this background that the explanation lies for Syria's cooperation with the US counter-terror effort, since much of that effort is directed against al-Qaida, which is militantly Islamic and Sunni in orientation. The Syrian regime is not al-Qaida's first target, but were al-Qaida or a force like it to hold sway in the Middle East, the authorities in Damascus would be among the losers.

At the end of World War I, Syria and Lebanon were placed under French authority. This was deeply unpopular and Syrian loathing of it escalated with every round of popular opposition and heavy-handed repression. After World War II, the USA, USSR and Britain recognized Syria's independence while France still claimed authority, and British Prime Minister Winston Churchill threatened to send British forces to uphold Syria's independence before France finally agreed to pull out.

In 1958 Syria joined Egypt in the United Arab Republic (UAR). The experience was not what had been anticipated. Egypt was by far the larger country, and Nasser's self-confidence and authority were enhanced by the 1956 Suez crisis and War. From a Syrian perspective, it seemed Nasser wanted a complete union of the two states, in which it

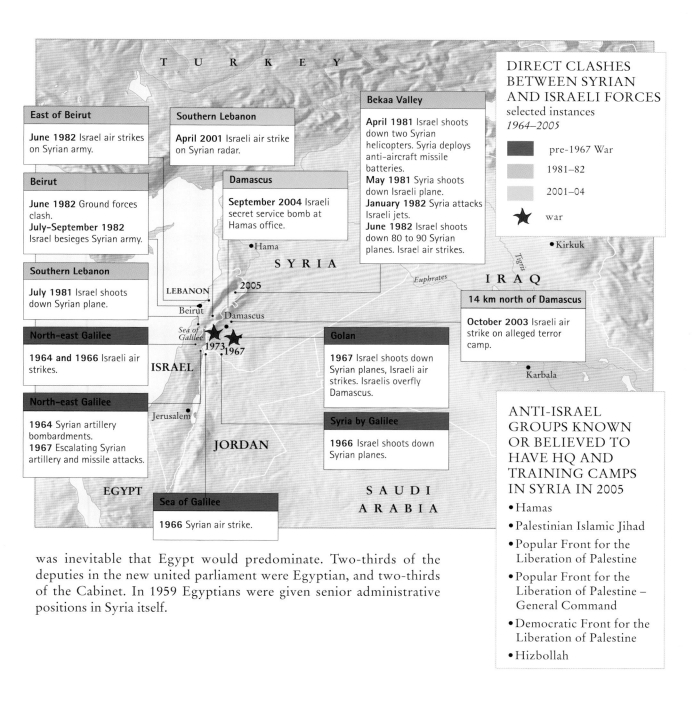

DIRECT CLASHES BETWEEN SYRIAN AND ISRAELI FORCES
selected instances
1964–2005

- pre-1967 War
- 1981–82
- 2001–04
- ★ war

East of Beirut

June 1982 Israel air strikes on Syrian army.

Southern Lebanon

April 2001 Israeli air strike on Syrian radar.

Bekaa Valley

April 1981 Israel shoots down two Syrian helicopters. Syria deploys anti-aircraft missile batteries.
May 1981 Syria shoots down Israeli plane.
January 1982 Syria attacks Israeli jets.
June 1982 Israel shoots down 80 to 90 Syrian planes. Israel air strikes.

Beirut

June 1982 Ground forces clash.
July–September 1982 Israel besieges Syrian army.

Damascus

September 2004 Israeli secret service bomb at Hamas office.

Southern Lebanon

July 1981 Israel shoots down Syrian plane.

14 km north of Damascus

October 2003 Israeli air strike on alleged terror camp.

North-east Galilee

1964 and 1966 Israeli air strikes.

Golan

1967 Israel shoots down Syrian planes, Israeli air strikes. Israelis overfly Damascus.

North-east Galilee

1964 Syrian artillery bombardments.
1967 Escalating Syrian artillery and missile attacks.

Syria by Galilee

1966 Israel shoots down Syrian planes.

Sea of Galilee

1966 Syrian air strike.

ANTI-ISRAEL GROUPS KNOWN OR BELIEVED TO HAVE HQ AND TRAINING CAMPS IN SYRIA IN 2005

- Hamas
- Palestinian Islamic Jihad
- Popular Front for the Liberation of Palestine
- Popular Front for the Liberation of Palestine – General Command
- Democratic Front for the Liberation of Palestine
- Hizbollah

was inevitable that Egypt would predominate. Two-thirds of the deputies in the new united parliament were Egyptian, and two-thirds of the Cabinet. In 1959 Egyptians were given senior administrative positions in Syria itself.

POLITICS, FORCE AND RISK

A military coup levered Syria out of the UAR in 1961, and there followed a decade of instability and sometimes chaos, with a succession of coups and counter-coups. There was a period in 1962 when it was unclear if the elected national assembly actually existed.

Despite the experience of the UAR, the Ba'athist emphasis on Arab unity was still influential and in 1963 the Ba'athists came to power. However, the party was itself riven by different interpretations of unity. In patterns that were also characteristic of politics in Egypt and Iraq, there was a dispute between those who emphasized pan-Arab unity above other allegiances, and those who emphasized the needs and interests of Syria. Alongside disputes around this issue, arguments over economic and social development led to division between factions with more and less socialist domestic programmes.

The key founders of Ba'athism – Michel Aflaq and Salah al-Din al-Bitar – were expelled from the Syrian Ba'ath Party in 1966. This marked the end of a process by which the military wing of the party – that is, the part of the Ba'ath Party that was within the Syrian military – steadily weakened the civilian leadership's capacity to lead, and finally supplanted it. It also marked a move away from the pan-Arab aspirations towards a Syrian focus in party ideology.

The new regime was increasingly radical and active against Israel. It intensified the pressure of guerrilla attacks on Israel while its diplomatic and political pressure forced Egypt into ever more confrontational mode with Israel to maintain its leadership within the Arab world. The policy successfully escalated the conflict but culminated in June 1967 in another catastrophic Arab defeat by Israel, which included the loss of Syrian territory in the Golan Heights.

The regime's authority was fatally weakened by the defeat in the 1967 Six-Day War. General Hafez al-Assad had been rising in influence and prestige in the mid-1960s and with the 1966 coup had received the post of Minister of Defence. Yet he managed to evade the blame for the defeat, which somewhat paradoxically perhaps was the catalyst for his further rise. A further Syrian military fiasco was the background to the final coup in 1970. In the factional maelstrom of Ba'athist politics within the armed forces, Assad controlled the air force but not the army. When open fighting broke out between the PLO and the Jordanian government in September 1970, the Syrian government wanted to intervene on the PLO's side. Assad disagreed because of the risk of Israeli or even US intervention. So when Syrian tank forces went into Jordan, Assad refused to provide air cover, and the tanks were accordingly driven back by the Jordanians. Less than two months later, the Ba'athist Party congress supported the government and criticized Assad and others, but to no avail. The day after the congress ended, in a bloodless coup, Assad assumed power. Confirmed in office by a referendum in 1971, he stayed in power until his death, and was succeeded by his son.

From 1977 onwards, Lebanon joined Israel as a pre-eminent foreign policy and security issue for Syria. Whereas Israel and the western multinational forces were forced out of Lebanon, Syria stayed. It defined the terms of the agreement that ended the war in Lebanon, and it defined its own dominant role. In early 2005, Rafik al-Hariri, former Lebanese Prime Minister and an open opponent of Syrian influence in Lebanon, was assassinated. Syria was widely believed to have organized the killing, even if it was also widely thought likely that this was the work of a faction rather than the government as a whole. An independent UN report concluded that senior Syrian officials were indeed behind the murder. The pressure on Syria to terminate its military presence in Lebanon was overwhelming.

Though Syria withdrew its regular military forces from Lebanon in 2005, that is not the same as abandoning all attempts to control Lebanese politics and shape the government. It has other means of influence and there was no sign of any fundamental rethinking by the Syrian leadership of the relationship with Lebanon. The Syrian role in the war and occupation held back its economy, and according to UN definitions and data 30 percent of Syrians live below the poverty line. Nonetheless, Syria has not given up playing an important regional role and is not deterred by the risks involved.

Taking risks in regional politics is an integral part of Syrian policy. The systematic way it set about escalating conflict with Israel in 1966, leading directly to the Six Day War in 1967, is the archetype. For years, it had tense and openly hostile relations with Turkey to its north and permitted the Kurdistan Workers Party – the PKK – to have its headquarters in Syria as it pursued its war against Turkey. Likewise, Syria and Iraq had an intensely antagonistic relationship, partly because the two regimes emerged from rival wings of Ba'athism. Since 1999, Syria has pragmatically eased relations with Turkey, but Bashar al-Assad has shown no greater will to compromise with Israel than his father did and continues to allow opponents of Israel to operate within Syria. In 2003 Israel made its first air attack on Syria since the 1973 war, and in 2004 a political assassination in Damascus was attributed to the Israeli secret service. With the US occupation of Iraq starting in 2003, new risks emerged: neither US success nor success for the insurgents linked to al-Qaida would be to Syria's liking, and nor is perpetual chaos in Iraq in its interests.

Some states might respond to this catalogue of danger by opting for a quiet, non-assertive policy. Syria's response has always been activist and assertive, which means that it deliberately and knowingly continues to walk a dangerous line. It remains deeply involved in Lebanon, despite withdrawing its forces in 2005 after ex-PM Hariri was murdered and continues to host anti-Israeli militants. A senior Hizbollah figure was killed in February 2008 in Damascus. He allegedly planned the 1983 Beirut bombs against the international forces, and the kidnap of two Israeli soldiers in 2006 that sparked the war that year. Who was responsible was not clear but the danger was.

MILITARY COUPS AND THEIR LEADERS
since independence in 1944

1949 March	Brigadier General Husni az Zaim
August	Brigadier General al-Hinnawi
December	Colonel Adib al-Shishakhli
1954 February	Senior officers in favour of civilian rule
1961 December	Senior officers opposed to union with Egypt: Nazim al-Qudsi elected President
1962 March	General Command of the army and armed forces
April	Supporters of al-Qudsi
1963 January	(failed) most of the 1962 coup-makers
March	Salah al-Din al-Bitar
July	(failed) 2,000 Nasserite officers
1966 February	General al-Salah al-Jadid, General Hafez al-Assad and Nureddin Atassi
1970 November	General Hafez al-Assad

LIBYA

As leader of Libya since the coup he led, aged 27, to overthrow the monarchy in 1969, Muammar Qadhafi has espoused a militant pan-Arabism, attempting to claim the mantle of President Nasser of Egypt who died in 1970. With a population less than one-twelfth of Egypt's, Qadhafi's ambition for leadership in the Arab world and in Africa has always been greater than his capacity. He could never get much more than purely rhetorical support for essentially anachronistic attempts to unify Arab states in the 1970s and later. And his radical anti-US policies and support for violent revolution are not to the taste of most Arab leaders. Nonetheless he has been a more serious and influential figure than many western commentators have been prepared to acknowledge. His support for the formation of the African Union has been regarded as particularly influential in Africa, while the secular basis of his politics continues to provide an alternative kind of anti-Americanism to that promoted by the Islamist movements of the Middle East.

After the 1969 coup, Qadhafi launched the cultural revolution in 1973 and a people's revolution in 1977 as expressions of his 'Third Universal Theory' of direct democracy and popular control of the state, which is neither Marxist nor capitalist. He has never persuaded foreign observers, however, that his three decades and more in power were attributable to anything but the usual apparatus of personalized state control, which included both the media and direct repression. In the mid-1990s uncertain reports surfaced of violent conflict inside Libya.

Libyan foreign policy focused primarily on two things: the Israeli-Palestinian conflict, in which it took a position against any compromise on eliminating outside influence on the Arab world; and the export of revolution. Support was given not only to the PLO, until it tried to make peace with Israel with the Oslo Accord in 1993, and other groups in the Middle East but also, for example, to the IRA in the form of training and supplies. The policy led to direct confrontation with the USA, culminating in the 1986 bombing of Libya in the wake of a bomb in a Berlin nightclub in which many Americans were wounded. A few years later came international political isolation when evidence linked Libya to the death of 270 people on board PanAm flight 103, which was blown up in mid-air over Lockerbie, Scotland.

However, there is no evidence of links between Libya and the al-Qaida network, despite their common ground of uncompromising opposition to Israel, the USA and foreign influence in the Middle East. In 2004, Libya arrested 17 al-Qaida suspects and had by then been working actively against the network for several years. Though the issues are unclear to outsiders, it seems that al-Qaida's network may include groups of Libyans who fought in Afghanistan and who, on their return, sought Qadhafi's overthrow.

In the late 1990s, Qadhafi adopted a pragmatic foreign policy that began steadily to erode Libya's isolation. Handing over the Lockerbie suspects (one was convicted, one acquitted), acknowledging responsibility, agreeing US$ 2.7 billion compensation and terminating its programme to develop weapons of mass destruction allowed Libya back to international normality. The end of UN sanctions – and of the separate sanctions imposed by the USA – has raised the prospect of increased international investment in Libyan oil. About 75 percent of government revenue comes from oil exports but there has been no oil prospecting in much of the country, so there could be new discoveries and increased revenues to come.

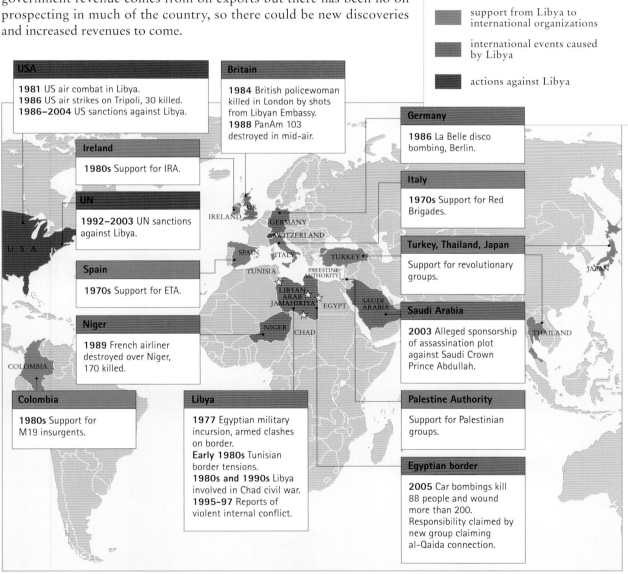

LIBYA AND THE WORLD
1995–2004

☆ internal and border clashes

support from Libya to international organizations

international events caused by Libya

actions against Libya

USA

1981 US air combat in Libya.
1986 US air strikes on Tripoli, 30 killed.
1986–2004 US sanctions against Libya.

Britain

1984 British policewoman killed in London by shots from Libyan Embassy.
1988 PanAm 103 destroyed in mid-air.

Germany

1986 La Belle disco bombing, Berlin.

Ireland

1980s Support for IRA.

Italy

1970s Support for Red Brigades.

UN

1992–2003 UN sanctions against Libya.

Turkey, Thailand, Japan

Support for revolutionary groups.

Spain

1970s Support for ETA.

Saudi Arabia

2003 Alleged sponsorship of assassination plot against Saudi Crown Prince Abdullah.

Niger

1989 French airliner destroyed over Niger, 170 killed.

Colombia

1980s Support for M19 insurgents.

Libya

1977 Egyptian military incursion, armed clashes on border.
Early 1980s Tunisian border tensions.
1980s and 1990s Libya involved in Chad civil war.
1995–97 Reports of violent internal conflict.

Palestine Authority

Support for Palestinian groups.

Egyptian border

2005 Car bombings kill 88 people and wound more than 200. Responsibility claimed by new group claiming al-Qaida connection.

Map labels: U S A, COLOMBIA, IRELAND, UK, SPAIN, TUNISIA, ITALY, GERMANY, SWITZERLAND, LIBYAN ARAB JAMAHIRIYA, NIGER, CHAD, EGYPT, PALESTINE AUTHORITY, TURKEY, SAUDI ARABIA, THAILAND, JAPAN

EGYPT

With over 77 million people, Egypt is the most populous Arab country. Its size, strategic location, cultural and intellectual output and history combine to make it the traditional centre of the Arab world. For most Arabs, it was fitting that, under President Nasser, Egypt should claim leadership, and not only because of his success in the Suez crisis. Therefore, it was an especially deep betrayal that under Sadat Egypt should make peace with Israel, and under Mubarak should be closely allied with the USA.

As US policy became more closely supportive of Israel during the 1960s, so Nasser, despite being one of the leaders of the group of states opting for non-alignment between East and West, turned increasingly to the USSR for economic, political and military support. But when Nasser was manoeuvred by Syria into a more intense confrontation with Israel that led to the disastrous 1967 war, many of the claims of his presidency began to look somewhat shallow. Crucially, the country lagged in economic and social development, liberties were highly restricted, and Israel flourished. When Nasser died, his successor soon sought a wholly new direction, at least in relation to Israel.

It was Nasser's over-riding commitment to pan-Arab solidarity that had trapped him into the build-up to the 1967 war. It had put the policy initiative into the militant and risk-taking hands of Syria *(see page 52)*. A new policy towards Israel therefore meant a turn away from Nasser's core international policies and the opposition this would generate among other Arab leaders had to be balanced by finding new friends in the West.

The 1973 war was launched by Sadat to strengthen his position against Israel and buy diplomatic room for manoeuvre to undertake an epochal change, beginning the process of aligning Egypt with the West, making peace with Israel along the way, and opening economic doors to western trade and investment in order to boost development.

Nasser's period in office had somewhat blunted his radicalism at home during the 1960s. Sadat took the economic conservatism and pragmatism further. This generated stiffening opposition from the left, who were only partially won over by Egypt's relative success in the 1973 war – or, less charitably and more precisely, the lesser degree of failure compared to 1967. As Sadat started to align with some US policies, the socialist opposition grew stronger and angrier. To weaken the leftist opposition, Sadat took the fateful step of quietly providing practical support and semi-official tolerance to the Muslim Brotherhood and newer Islamist groups. They, however, were equally outraged by the growing accommodation with Israel and the USA. And not only did they oppose Sadat's economic policies at home, Islamist groups also began to develop practical welfare programmes which did something to look after the urban poor. As the 1970s passed, the Islamist opposition became the main internal challenge to the government.

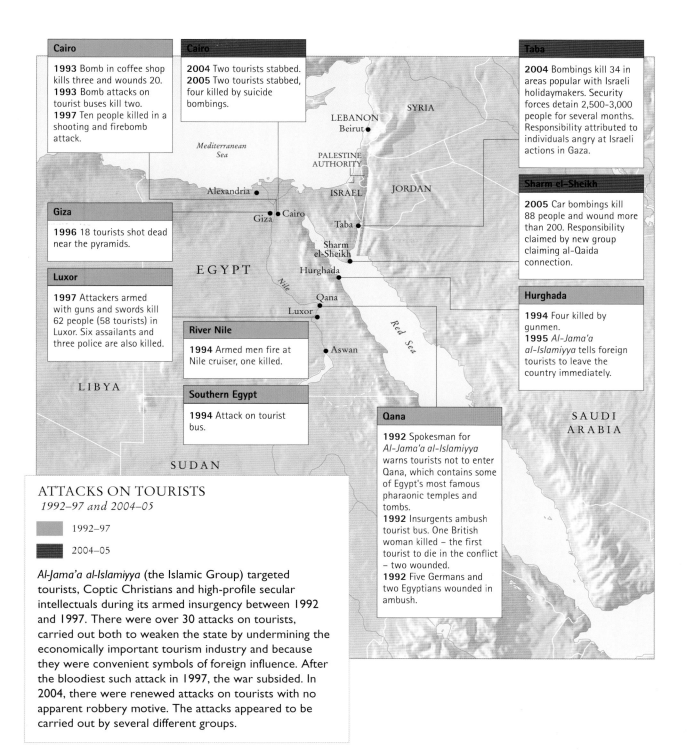

Cairo

1993 Bomb in coffee shop kills three and wounds 20.
1993 Bomb attacks on tourist buses kill two.
1997 Ten people killed in a shooting and firebomb attack.

Cairo

2004 Two tourists stabbed.
2005 Two tourists stabbed, four killed by suicide bombings.

Taba

2004 Bombings kill 34 in areas popular with Israeli holidaymakers. Security forces detain 2,500-3,000 people for several months. Responsibility attributed to individuals angry at Israeli actions in Gaza.

Sharm el–Sheikh

2005 Car bombings kill 88 people and wound more than 200. Responsibility claimed by new group claiming al-Qaida connection.

Giza

1996 18 tourists shot dead near the pyramids.

Hurghada

1994 Four killed by gunmen.
1995 *Al-Jama'a al-Islamiyya* tells foreign tourists to leave the country immediately.

Luxor

1997 Attackers armed with guns and swords kill 62 people (58 tourists) in Luxor. Six assailants and three police are also killed.

River Nile

1994 Armed men fire at Nile cruiser, one killed.

Southern Egypt

1994 Attack on tourist bus.

Qana

1992 Spokesman for *Al-Jama'a al-Islamiyya* warns tourists not to enter Qana, which contains some of Egypt's most famous pharaonic temples and tombs.
1992 Insurgents ambush tourist bus. One British woman killed – the first tourist to die in the conflict – two wounded.
1992 Five Germans and two Egyptians wounded in ambush.

ATTACKS ON TOURISTS
1992–97 and 2004–05

▨ 1992–97

▨ 2004–05

Al-Jama'a al-Islamiyya (the Islamic Group) targeted tourists, Coptic Christians and high-profile secular intellectuals during its armed insurgency between 1992 and 1997. There were over 30 attacks on tourists, carried out both to weaken the state by undermining the economically important tourism industry and because they were convenient symbols of foreign influence. After the bloodiest such attack in 1997, the war subsided. In 2004, there were renewed attacks on tourists with no apparent robbery motive. The attacks appeared to be carried out by several different groups.

73

THE RISE OF ISLAMIST POLITICS

In the 1920s Egypt had been the birthplace of the Muslim Brotherhood, which became a major force, providing welfare services for ordinary people and challenging the nationalists for political support in the 1940s. It assisted in the Free Officers' revolution in 1952 but was then banned in 1954. In the years that followed, despite having been banned, the Muslim Brothers remained a dynamic social force and in response to their partial suppression more radical groups – often more willing to use violence – attracted growing numbers of recruits. The writings of Sayyid Qutb, who was executed by the Egyptian government in 1966, were particularly influential; he denounced the state as impious and advocated its violent overthrow.

In the wake of the 1967 war, some Egyptian commentators and other Arab writers noted that what they perceived to be a religious state – Israel – had won a humiliating victory over the secular Arab states. For these writers, the Arabs could only turn the tide by reconnecting their religion with their politics. At the same time, in the long Arab discussion about how best to relate to the West – by copying it, or by borrowing from it what is compatible with Islam, or by rejecting it – the increasingly Islamist tone of political debate leaned towards rejection, leavened by a very selective borrowing of the West's technological accomplishments. Sadat's tactical encouragement of the Islamists in the late 1970s helped strengthen the position of an already strong, self-confident movement that rejected root and branch every item of his economic and political agenda and the legitimacy of the state he led.

When Sadat was assassinated by Islamist militants in 1981, Mubarak continued his policies. By then, the realignment with the USA and peace with Israel were complete, and Egypt had been excluded from the Arab League which it had co-founded and whose headquarters it hosted. This exclusion could not last; Egypt is too central in Arab affairs and has too much political, diplomatic and military weight to be sidelined for long. Eventually, its close ties with the West were part of the reason why its reintegration into the Arab political world was welcomed by those who earlier inveighed against its compromise with Israel.

When Iraq invaded Kuwait in 1990, there is some evidence that Mubarak, like some other Arab leaders, viewed it as a limited move that offered no wider threat, not even to Saudi Arabia. He was therefore, some reports indicate, inclined not to express outright condemnation. But when the US-led coalition drove Iraqi forces out of Kuwait, there was an Egyptian contingent present that saw combat and suffered casualties. To encourage Mubarak to join the anti-Iraq coalition, the USA cancelled $7 billion of debt, while other western governments forgave a further $5-10 billion between them, and Arab creditors wiped out $6.5 billion in debt and agreed to provide about $2 billion in direct grants. Much of the debt to the USA had been incurred buying American weapons.

That episode apart, it is hard to argue that Mubarak has had any more success on the economic front than Sadat. Economic growth has not been fast enough to meet the needs of a growing population. Indebtedness is high again and meanwhile, longer-term and more profound problems are looming, while rapid population growth may soon put too much demand on the water of the Nile, along which the vast majority of Egypt's population is clustered.

Mubarak's diplomacy has been less high-octane than Sadat's; the key problem of peace with Israel had already been solved. He has been adroit at being a good American ally while maintaining significant distance over some issues, such as the second US-Iraq war in 2003. And the peace agreement with Israel has not prevented him from voicing strong criticisms of Israeli actions and policies. In fact, Mubarak's foreign policy in relation to Israel and the USA is not very different from that of many western European states; an ally of the USA but with growing disillusionment, and a critic of Israel but without taking action against it.

Within Egypt, the period of Mubarak's leadership has been a permanent state of emergency, as declared following Sadat's assassination. Islamic political organizations are banned and secular political parties cannot operate without being officially approved. The Muslim Brotherhood is informally tolerated but its ability to participate in politics is strictly limited.

The potential for violence exploded in 1992 into five years of armed conflict in which about 1,000 people were killed, and during which the tourism trade was a particular target. In response, the Egyptian authorities have been willing to take harsh measures, especially since the Luxor massacre in 1997, which was effectively the last act of the internal war. The return from 2004 on, of political violence against tourists – defined as violent incidents in which robbery is not evidently the motive – indicated the continuing possibility of a social and political explosion in Egypt. It was not clear that this was a return of the conflict of the 1990s; the perpetrators and their motives appeared to be varied. One major incident was attributed to anger against Israel, while another was claimed by a group that announced it had al-Qaida connections. The response to the 2004 Taba bombing, which saw thousands of suspects arrested, showed that the government remained committed to draconian measures if deemed necessary.

Egypt has a young population – 49 percent are below the age of 18 – and its economic problems continue while its political system frustrates demands for change. These three factors combined are a recipe for risk, with further ingredients in Gaza. In response to missile attacks by Gaza militants on Israeli villages, Israel closed the border crossings in 2007-08, triggering a humanitarian crisis. Militants blew a huge hole in the Egyptian border wall and tens of thousands of Palestinians poured through it seeking food and medical supplies. It is the guile and determination of Egypt's political leaders and security forces that provide stability, not any sureness in the country's social and economic foundations. That kind of stability is inherently fragile.

ALGERIA

In Algeria's civil war from 1992 to 2003, the insurgents were militant Islamists but it was not a religious war. It originated in the political and economic flaws of Algeria's development since independence and caused the death of 150,000 people.

Democracy did not survive long after independence. Ahmed Ben Bella was elected President in 1963; two years later, Chief of Staff Houari Boumédienne took power and Ben Bella spent the next 14 years under house arrest. Under Boumédienne, Algeria was both a one-party state and dominated by the military, a system that combined two rigid forms of government, each of which ruled out adaptation as a response to crises. When the economy was successful, as it was through the 1970s, buoyed by rising oil prices, the system worked. When oil revenues fell in the mid-1980s, dissatisfaction rose and the system was too rigid to cope. Unrest culminated, in 1988, in four days of rioting with hundreds killed.

This weakened the authorities' confidence and unity, and the government decided on a democratic experiment. New political parties were permitted. But the government was still dominated by the military and its heart was in the one-party model.

The wealth of the privileged elite that ran the once revolutionary FLN party was in sharp contrast to the privations of the masses. Protests were driven by moral outrage as well as hardship, and the moral clarity of a political party that urged a return to the basic values of Islam turned out to have a broad appeal in Algerian society. In 1990, just one year after being formed, the Islamic Salvation Front (FIS) won over half the votes in local elections.

The problem for the government was how to have democracy without letting the majority win. In June 1991 it announced parliamentary elections, tightened the rules to disadvantage FIS and arrested its two most prominent leaders. Nonetheless at the end of the year, FIS dominated the first election round and was clearly heading for victory, perhaps even with enough seats that it could change the constitution and establish an Islamic state. At the beginning of 1992, the military stepped in, cancelled the second round, replaced the President and suspended political rights. There was now no avenue for peaceful change.

Western governments regarded anything as better than the Islamists taking power and quietly backed the military, as did most Arab governments. But FIS resisted. Initial attacks targeted security forces. In a few months, some insurgent factions started attacking civilians, and in 1993 the GIA was formed by veterans of the war in Afghanistan to oppose FIS outright as well as the government. It targeted anybody who supported or worked for the government and attacked foreigners, driving them out and leaving the country virtually isolated. Late in 1994, guerrilla groups loyal to FIS but hitherto divided among themselves agreed to bury their differences and formed the AIS.

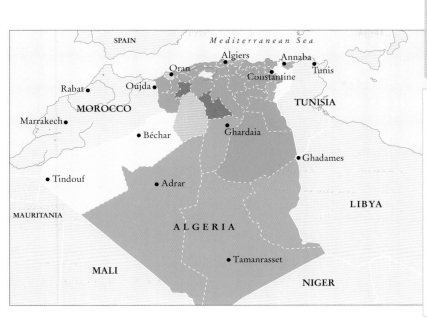

Political organizations
FLN — National Liberation Front
FIS — Islamic Salvation Front
GIA — Armed Islamic Group
AIS — Islamic Salvation Army
GSPC — Salafist Group for Preaching
and Combat

OPPOSITION ELECTION DOMINANCE
Parliamentary election results 1991

Just two years after opposition parties were permitted, the Islamic Salvation Front (FIS) dominated the first round of elections.

FIS majority vote

50% FIS

non-FIS majority

undecided

no data

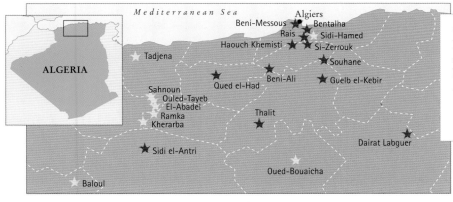

CIVILIAN MASSACRES
Incidents in which
more than 50 people killed
by Armed Islamic Group (GIA)
1997–98

★ 1997 ★ 1998

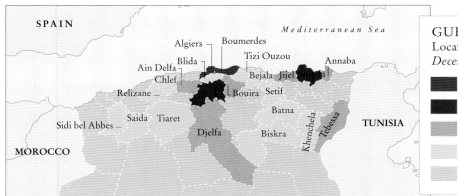

GUERRILLA ATTACKS
Location by province
December 2004–September 2005

9 or over

6 to 8

3 to 5

2 or under

none or no data

77

CHRONOLOGY *continued*

1994 Armed groups loyal to FIS form AIS. Newly appointed President Liamine Zéroual begins negotiations with FIS.

1995 Presidential elections confirm Zéroual in office. GIA and AIS fight each other.

1997 Parliamentary elections won by pro-Zéroual National Democratic Rally.

1997–98 War dominated by GIA's massacres of civilians.

1997 AIS declares unilateral ceasefire.

1998 Formation of GSPC – a breakaway group from the GIA.

1999 Former foreign minister Abdelaziz Bouteflika elected president with no opposition. Amnesty offered to Islamist fighters. Thousands pardoned.

2000 AIS disbands.

2001 Over 100 Berber demonstrators killed by security forces.

2002 President Bouteflika announces that the Berber language, Tamazight, is to be recognized as a national language.

June Prime Minister Ali Benflis's FLN wins general election marred by violence, low turnout and boycott by four parties. GIA leader dies, group incapacitated.

2003 GSPC continues assassinating police and army personnel. Declares support for al-Qaida.

2004 President Bouteflika is re-elected to a second term in landslide victory.

2005 Government-commissioned report says security forces were responsible for disappearances of over 6,000 people. Referendum backs wider amnesty and compensation for families of victims of government forces.

2006 GSPC renames itself as al-Qaida in the Islamic Maghreb. Attacks police station.

2007 Bomb attacks on army police, foreign workers, UN staff, law courts and other targets .

Amid war, there were attempts to find peace. Though the newly appointed president, Liamine Zéroual, supported a hard line in army operations, he held talks with FIS in 1994. Most of the opposition groups came together for a new political initiative in 1995. The same year saw multi-party elections, won by Zéroual with 60 percent of votes cast. Despite a boycott by FIS and the GIA's threat to kill anybody who voted – its slogan at the time was 'one vote, one bullet' – turnout was about 76 percent.

In 1997, the GIA launched a series of massacres for which it openly claimed credit. These targeted entire villages or neighbourhoods, and areas near Algiers that had voted heavily for FIS in 1990 and 1991 were particularly chosen for attack.

Their justification for this appears to have been that those who were not actively fighting the government were corrupt beyond redemption. Makeshift weapons such as mattocks and shovels were used as well as guns and knives. GIA fighters dismembered men one limb at a time, sliced open pregnant women, dashed children against walls and kidnapped young women for sexual slavery. In some of the worst massacres government forces stationed nearby did nothing to save the victims.

Throughout the war, government security forces were also responsible for serious abuse of human rights. Mass graves of people who had been 'disappeared' have been discovered since the fighting stopped.

There were three parties to the war: the government, the GIA and the AIS/FIS, plus a host of smaller factions of unclear loyalty. In late 1997, the AIS announced a unilateral ceasefire and, in 1998, the GIA split: the new GSPC was formed by ex-GIA fighters, who opposed the massacres and focused their attacks on the army and police.

These developments slowly opened the way for a new peace effort. When Zéroual stepped down in 1999, the army supported Abdelaziz Bouteflika, who stood for election unopposed because of other candidates' and parties' concerns about the high risk of electoral fraud. Bouteflika opened negotiations with the AIS, leading to an agreement on amnesty. The AIS disbanded the following year. The army concentrated on destroying the GIA and, from several thousand fighters in the mid-1990s, the group was down to about 60 by 2003. The number of war-deaths each year fell from over 10,000 at peak in the 1990s, to 1,900 in 2001, 1,400 in 2002 and 900 in 2003. Slowly but not always steadily, there was a sense of some normality returning, but the 2002 elections were marred by violence and the GSPC was still active in 2004 and 2005, with about 300 fighters.

Yet as the civil war seemed to be dying down, the GSPC linked itself to a wider conflict agenda by declaring its allegiance to al-Qaida, changing its name and opening up a new round of escalation beginning in October 2006. The group's new energy threatened the country's fragile but distinctly emerging sense of peace and future prospects. Whether there would be a return to repression and terror, however, was not clear.

The Berbers in Algeria

As far back as there are records of North Africa, there is evidence of Berbers. They comprise several ethnic groups, which official statistics often treat as an indistinguishable part of an Arab-Berber population. Most Berbers are Muslims, their forbears having converted at the time of the Arab conquests, but many Berber customs survive and they remain an identifiably separate group.

The Berber languages – collectively known as Tamazight – are spoken by some 25 million people, of whom about 20 million live in Morocco and Algeria. There are 7–10 million Berbers in Algeria, about 20–30 percent of the population.

In the 19th and 20th centuries, Berbers were the main source of resistance to French colonialism. The heart of the guerrilla struggle in the first phase of the war of independence from 1954 was in Berber areas, and in 1957 four out of nine FLN leaders were Berbers.

Many politically active Berbers concluded that independence in 1962 did not bring them the rewards they anticipated, which were instead monopolized by the urban Arab elite that dominated the FLN at that time. In 1963, a Berber uprising, demanding improved rights, started and lasted for two years.

In 1980, in events that came to be known as the 'Berber Spring', the banning of a lecture on ancient Berber poetry sparked protests, mainly by students. The government's harsh response led to a death toll variously reported as between 30 and 100. There was more campus unrest on the anniversary of the 'Spring' in 1981 and 1985. The demand was for Tamazight to be an official national language. The FLN, however, demanded cultural and political uniformity and in 1981 codified Algerian identity as a product of Arab and Islamic civilization, thus denying the acknowledgement and, by implication, the rights that Berbers sought.

In the midst of civil war in 1995, the Rome-based Sant' Egidio Community facilitated an agreement between most Algerian opposition groups – excluding the GIA – which expressed a shared view of the Algeria they hoped for after the war. As well as an emphasis on democracy, human rights and post-war justice, a key element of the agreement was acknowledging Berbers, Arabs and the Islamic faith as all being essential aspects of Algerian national identity.

As the civil war tailed off, there was renewed Berber activism. Violent confrontation in 2001, around the anniversary of the 1980 Berber Spring, was this time known as 'Black Spring' as 120 people died and 2,000 were injured in protests demanding autonomy in the Berber area of Kabylia. The following year, President Bouteflika announced that Tamazight would be recognized as a national language. Since then it has been taught in schools and there have been promises of more support for economic development in Berber areas. Complaints remain among Berbers, however, about widespread discrimination, reflected in high unemployment rates.

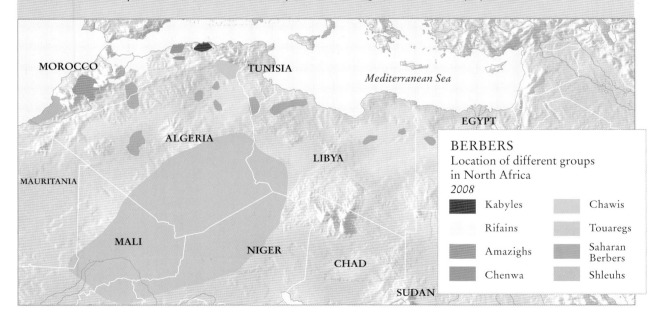

BERBERS
Location of different groups
in North Africa
2008

Kabyles
Rifains
Amazighs
Chenwa
Chawis
Touaregs
Saharan Berbers
Shleuhs

IRAN

In the 1970s, the West saw Iran as an island of stability in a volatile region. In reality, it was a classic case for revolution and it has remained a revolutionary state since 1979 when it became an Islamic Republic. Western observers were surprised that the revolution had a religious leader, but there was a precedent. Near the end of the 19th century, the Shah, close to bankruptcy, tried to raise cash by selling the British company Imperial Tobacco the monopoly rights to the tobacco harvest; the country's leading Ayatollah launched a non-smoking protest and the Shah reversed his decision.

There was always a deep opposition in the Iranian population to control by outside powers – primarily by Britain and the USA, with involvement from Russia and later the USSR. In the 1940s, a movement arose for national ownership of Iran's oil led by Mohammad Mossadeq; he became Prime Minister and would have won against the Shah had it not been for US and British intervention. As a result, the Shah was seen by many Iranians as the instrument of outside powers wishing to control Iran.

After the 1953 coup, the Shah centralized power and built up the state's repressive apparatus. As well as using coercion, he sought consent through economic development and reforms, but his efforts were hampered by corruption, inefficiency and his own unpopularity.

The country was changing in the 1950s and 1960s. Higher education expanded dramatically and, in particular, people moved to the cities. Urbanization helped change the role of mullahs in society, bringing them closer to the people, who wanted their advice to handle problems arising from changes in the basic terms of daily life.

In the early 1960s, Ruhollah Khomeini emerged as one of the foremost religious leaders. In 1962, he was arrested for criticizing a proposal to give US military personnel immunity from prosecution (a standard US requirement for its forces in foreign countries). The following year he was imprisoned for several months. There were huge demonstrations in his support, which were violently suppressed with 600 people killed and 2,000 injured. He was exiled in 1964 but not silenced. In Najaf, southern Iraq, from 1965 until 1978, he taught in a theological college, to which many young Iranian mullahs came; his sermons were taped and distributed on cassettes to large audiences in Iran.

In 1971, the Shah spent about $300 million celebrating what he claimed was 2,500 years of monarchy in Iran. Many thought the extravagance typical. That same year Khomeini published his argument for an Islamic government, and there were attacks on government targets by small Marxist and Islamist guerrilla groups.

Much of Iran's increased oil income in the mid-1970s was spent on arms from the USA. In 1976, shortages in basic foodstuffs started, affecting the middle class as well as the poor, and further undermining the Shah's remaining legitimacy.

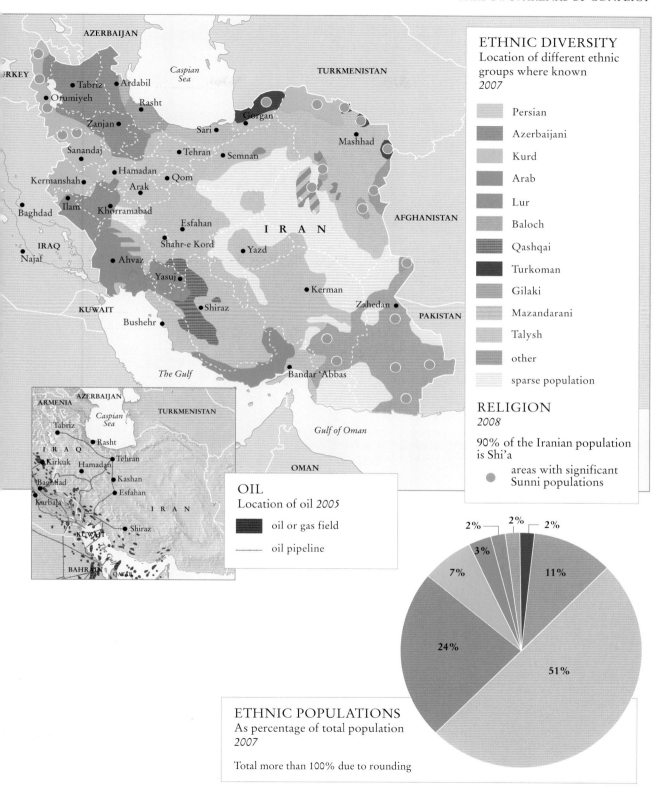

AZERBAIJAN

TURKEY

Caspian Sea

TURKMENISTAN

Tabriz • Ardabil

Orumiyeh

Rasht

Zanjan

Sanandaj

Sari

Gorgan

Semnan

Tehran

Mashhad

Kermanshah

Hamadan

Qom

Arak

Ilam Khorramabad

Baghdad

IRAQ

Najaf

Esfahan

Shahr-e Kord

I R A N

AFGHANISTAN

Yazd

KUWAIT

Ahvaz

Yasuj

Kerman

Shiraz

Zahedan

PAKISTAN

Bushehr

The Gulf

Bandar 'Abbas

Gulf of Oman

ETHNIC DIVERSITY
Location of different ethnic groups where known
2007

- Persian
- Azerbaijani
- Kurd
- Arab
- Lur
- Baloch
- Qashqai
- Turkoman
- Gilaki
- Mazandarani
- Talysh
- other
- sparse population

RELIGION
2008

90% of the Iranian population is Shi'a

● areas with significant Sunni populations

ARMENIA

AZERBAIJAN

Caspian Sea

TURKMENISTAN

Tabriz

Rasht

I R A Q

Kirkuk

Hamadan

Tehran

Baghdad

Kashan

Karbala

Esfahan

I R A N

KUWAIT

Shiraz

OMAN

BAHRAIN

QATAR

OIL
Location of oil *2005*

- oil or gas field
- ------- oil pipeline

ETHNIC POPULATIONS
As percentage of total population
2007

Total more than 100% due to rounding

2% 2% 2%

3%

7%

11%

24%

51%

REVOLUTION

The background for the 1979 revolution included hardship amid plenty, under a harsh and extravagant regime. There was a political history of resisting injustice, a cultural preference for fairness and equality, and a moral leader who voiced both the people's complaints and an alternative vision of government. In 1978, violent repression of demonstrations ignited cycles of renewed protest. In each protest, people were killed by the state security forces so each was followed by a 40-day mourning period, then a new protest with more killings. The Shah offered compromises but to no avail. Ill with cancer, he left the country in 1979. A few days later, Khomeini returned.

The Revolutionary Guards clamped down on opposition at home, with many arrests and later executions. Iran promised to spread Islamic revolution. It sent Revolutionary Guards to Lebanon to fight and from 1982 sponsored the new Hizbollah group. In Tehran, students backed by the government took US diplomats hostage, breaking the laws of inter-state relations.

But exporting revolution more widely had to wait. In 1980, Iraq seized on what seemed a moment of Iranian weakness and invaded, casting aside the 1975 agreement to share the Shatt al-Arab waterway. Eight years of war killed at least 300,000 Iranians, slashed oil exports and shattered the economy *(see pages 84–5)*. Eventually war fatigue pushed Iran into a cease-fire. Perhaps because of worry about this weakness, in the first months after the war Khomeini ordered wholesale execution of political prisoners. One estimate of the death toll by an Ayatollah who opposed the executions is 30,000.

In 1989 Iran broke international rules again: in the last year of his life Khomeini issued a *fatwa* against British writer Salman Rushdie, authorizing his assassination on the grounds that his novel *The Satanic Verses* was blasphemous. The revolution has created a system of government that seems to need persistent renewal of its insurgent energy at home and abroad, for if it loses momentum it risks toppling over.

In successive parliamentary elections, though all candidates are vetted by the Council of Guardians, the balance has swung between parties that seek continuing Islamic revolution and those who want less fervour and more personal freedom. The more moderate group won in 1992 and 2000, the revolutionaries in 1996 and 2004. And for two terms, 1997 to 2005, there was a reforming President in Mohammed Khatami. His inability to deliver economic improvement and the continuing restrictions on political freedoms led to harshly repressed demonstrations in 2003. In 2005, Mahmoud Ahmadinejad was elected President. Together with the *Majlis* majority, his policies offer limited economic liberalization while demanding political acquiescence and social conservatism. The key issue is whether he can deliver economic progress, which largely depends on generating new investment and relaxing the state's grip on large enterprises. Though the first three years of his presidency brought international prominence, the economy did not strengthen and public opinion began to sour.

Internationally, Ahmedinejad refreshed Iran's insurgent energy, breaking out of a deal with the EU under which Iran would not attempt to enrich uranium. He stated repeatedly that the technology was wanted only for nuclear energy. This is credible in principle because the technology for enriching uranium is basically the same whether the end product is for civil or military use. That means that much depends on the interpretation of motives. President Ahmedinejad undermined the credibility of his peaceful intentions by remarking that Israel should be destroyed, and followed up by denying that Jews had been mass murdered in Europe during World War II. Within months, the UN Security Council was insisting Iran stop uranium enrichment and the USA was apparently looking at the military option.

There was considerable unease in Iran's political religious elite about the president's predilection for risky policies and high profile stances. But Iran's regional influence was growing, partly as a consequence of the chaos in Iraq and the declining credibility of US policy. Some of the heat went out of the nuclear issue when the USA acknowledged that Iran probably did not have an active bomb-making programme.

But communication between Iran and the West remained full of mutual incomprehension. Most western governments seem not to understand why there was a revolution. Some Iranian leaders seem not to care about regional stability. The West finds it hard to take seriously a leader who denies the Jewish holocaust occurred, and many Iranians (and many Arabs) find it hard to acknowledge that such a denial simply ignores known facts. When communication is so poor, confrontation occurs easily and escalates fast.

THE IRANIAN DIASPORA
Iranians living outside Iran
late 1990s

 South Asia 100,000

 Asia/Pacific 120,000

 rest of the Middle East 190,000

 Iraq 250,000

 rest of the world 280,000

 Europe 405,000

 UAE & Bahrain 560,000

 Turkey 800,000

 USA 1,560,000

The Islamic Republic's Constitution

The Supreme Leader
Elected by the Assembly of Experts. Responsible for general policies, Commander-in-Chief, controls intelligence and security operations, has sole power to declare war. Appoints and dismisses the heads of the judiciary, state radio and television, and the commander of the Islamic Revolutionary Guard Corps. Appoints half the Council of Guardians.

The President
Elected by absolute majority of votes in popular ballot based on universal suffrage. Second only to Supreme Leader. Responsible for implementing the Constitution and leading the executive.

Parliament (*Majlis*)
290 members elected to a four-year term. It drafts legislation, ratifies international treaties, and approves the government budget.

The Assembly of Experts
Meets for one week every year, consists of 86 'virtuous and learned' clerics elected by the public to eight-year terms. Responsible for electing the Supreme Leader and has the authority to remove him.

The Council of Guardians
Composed of 12 jurists, six appointed by the Supreme Leader, six appointed by the *Majlis* on recommendation by the head of the judiciary. Responsible for interpreting the constitution, has power to veto laws passed by *Majlis* if they are inconsistent with Islamic Law. Vets candidates for elections.

The Expediency Council
Mediates disputes between *Majlis* and the Council of Guardians. Advises the Supreme Leader.

THE IRAN-IRAQ WAR

When Iraq invaded Iran in September 1980 Saddam Hussein probably had a double motive. First, to deal a pre-emptive blow to the new Islamic Republic of Iran; because Iraq was a state with a secular ideology and a large population of Shi'ites, he expected it to be top of the Iranian list for exporting the revolution. Second, to gain more power and influence in the region.

Iraq seemed set to win, with an army of 190,000 and 2,200 tanks; though Iran's air force still had the latest US combat aircraft, bought before the revolution, its army was weakened by purges of officers. Iraq's initial offensive seized Iranian territory near the border, but 200,000 Iranian volunteers strengthened the front lines and Iraq's gains were consequently limited.

Saddam was responsible for starting the war but Ayatollah Khomeini kept it going. Iran's Supreme Leader turned down successive cease-fire proposals and offers of negotiations. Once the initial offensive had been held back, his objective was not defensive – he aimed for the overthrow of Saddam Hussein.

Tactics were brutal. Both sides attacked cities. Iran compensated for a lack of tanks by throwing 'human waves' into its offensives. To begin with, they were volunteers, but one account from March 1984 tells of thousands of boys tied together with ropes and forced to attack through a minefield. And Iraq used chemical weapons (CW) – both mustard gas and nerve gas according to irrefutable, independent evidence.

The war extended to attacks on shipping in the Gulf. Although Iraq began the 'tanker war' and carried out most of the attacks, it was often Iran that was blamed by the West. By early 1988, eight navies from the region and ten from outside it were deployed in the Gulf to protect commercial shipping.

Iraq was supplied by France, the USSR and the USA. In February 1982, the Reagan administration removed Iraq from the list of terrorist countries and in November 1983 decided to work to prevent an Iraqi defeat. Its main assistance was economic – about $5 billion in commercial loans for agriculture and oil pipeline construction. The State Department knew Iraq was using CW routinely when Donald Rumsfeld visited Saddam to assure him officially of US support. US intelligence was given to Iraq to aid its military operations, including CW use. At the same time, the USA made overtures to Iran and secretly supplied it with weapons, hoping to make contact with less adamantly anti-US factions in the leadership, and to get Iranian assistance in tracing US hostages held by Shi'a groups in Lebanon. Some observers believe the US aim was to weaken both Iran and Iraq equally.

By the end of 1987 Iran's forces were seriously depleted while Iraq had been able to re-equip and its army had shown new levels of effectiveness. Further offensives in 1988 took the war back onto Iranian territory and

Iraqi missile attacks on Tehran caused 30 percent of the city's population to flee. In August, Khomeini took a decision he described as 'a cup of poison' and agreed at last to a cease-fire.

In terms of territory, everything returned to the pre-war position; no losses, no gains. In terms of people, at least half a million were dead, probably a million and some say as many as 1,500,000. And the economy of both countries was devastated.

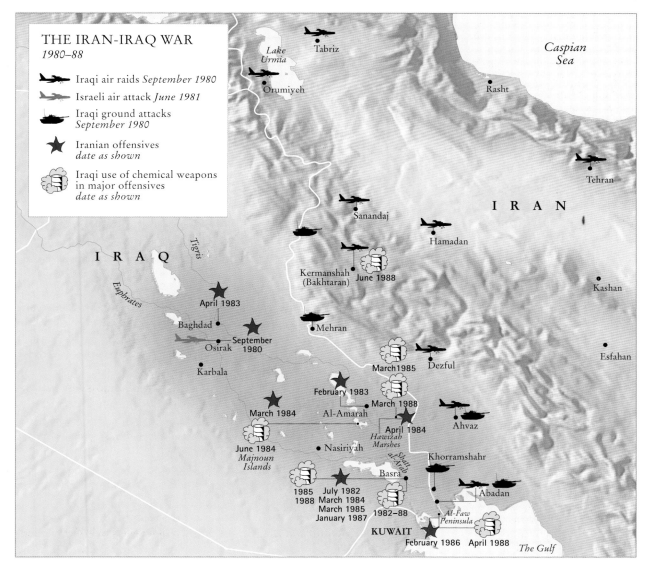

THE IRAN-IRAQ WAR
1980–88

Iraqi air raids *September 1980*

Israeli air attack *June 1981*

Iraqi ground attacks *September 1980*

Iranian offensives *date as shown*

Iraqi use of chemical weapons in major offensives *date as shown*

Lake Urmia

Tabriz

Orumiyeh

Rasht

Caspian Sea

Tehran

I R A N

Sanandaj

Hamadan

Kashan

Kermanshah (Bakhtaran)   June 1988

April 1983

Baghdad

September 1980

Osirak

Mehran

Esfahan

Karbala

March 1985   Dezful

February 1983

March 1984   Al-Amarah   March 1988

April 1984   Ahvaz

June 1984 *Majnoun Islands*

Nasiriyah   *Hawizah Marshes*

I R A Q

Tigris

Euphrates

Khorramshahr

1985
1988   July 1982
March 1984
March 1985
January 1987

Basra

1982–88

Abadan

Al-Faw Peninsula

Shatt al-Arab

KUWAIT

February 1986   April 1988

The Gulf

IRAQ

With about nine percent of the world's oil reserves and a population of 26 million, Iraq has the basic requirements for both prosperity and regional prominence. Its history since independence, however, has been marked by dictatorship, by internal, regional and international wars, and by extended periods of foreign control.

On the demise of the Ottoman Empire, Iraq was formed out of three imperial provinces. The country's history thus started as a dependent British territory, which is in reality how it remained until after World War II, despite formal independence in 1932. Though there were elections as early as 1925, Iraq has never been a democracy. Real power has always been in the hands of other states, various army factions or, for 35 years from 1968 to 2003, the Ba'ath Party.

Each of the three old Ottoman provinces that made up Iraq had its own history and identity; broadly, Kurdish in the north with large Assyrian and Turkoman minorities, Arab Sunni Muslim in the centre of the country, and Arab Shi'a Muslim in the south-east. Onto this patchwork, in 1921, the British brought an outsider to be king – Faisal, son of the Sharif of Mecca, commander in the Arab uprising against the Ottomans from 1916. The name al-Iraq that the British gave to the new mandate territory had previously been used for an area near Basra in the south. There was little basis for regarding Iraq as a unified country.

The lack of a common history and a unifying national consciousness did not make control by an outside power popular. In Iraq's first decade Britain held the country together and also held it down. In 1920, before Faisal was placed on the throne, there was an uprising against British domination by about 100,000 fighters. The British responded by bombing and strafing rebel villages. They have been widely accused of using poison gas weapons (not banned by treaty until 1925); though the evidence about this is not clear, there is no doubt that commanders in Iraq and the authorities in London considered the option.

The early years of Iraq's independence from 1932 were marked by political instability. The military moved onto the political stage in 1936 with a coup inspired by the model of Turkey under Kemal Atatürk. The monarchy remained in place throughout various upheavals; the appointment of a reforming cabinet, its removal by more conservative senior offices, and the successive governments made and re-made by this group over the next five years. In 1941 a pro-German army faction staged a coup; in response, Britain took over again.

In 1958 the monarchy was overthrown in a violent coup by a group inspired by the Free Officers' Movement in Egypt that had overthrown King Farouk six years earlier. Its leader Brigadier Qassem, became President. The coup had mass support but the Iraqi officers' movement lacked unity on two key issues – a programme for social and economic

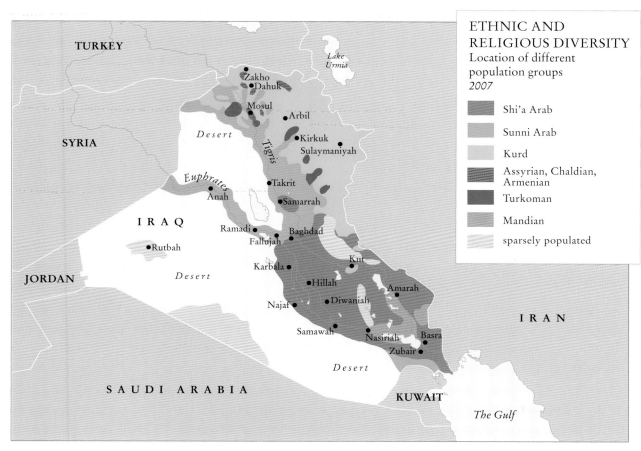

ETHNIC AND
RELIGIOUS DIVERSITY
Location of different
population groups
2007

Shi'a Arab

Sunni Arab

Kurd

Assyrian, Chaldian,
Armenian

Turkoman

Mandian

sparsely populated

development and Iraq's position in the Arab world. On the latter issue, the choice lay between the pan-Arab unity of Nasserism and an Iraq-first approach. Some officers wanted to join the United Arab Republic, newly formed by Egypt and Syria. But Iraq-first had strong support, including from the Iraqi Communist Party, which had flourished despite being banned under the monarchy, and could mobilize 500,000 supporters in demonstrations. For them, much of the point of the revolution was to be free of the influence of foreign leaders and outside powers.

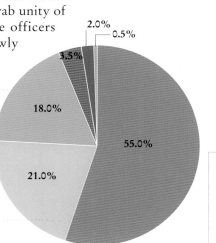

POPULATION
GROUPS
As percentage
of total population
2007

THE BA'ATH PARTY

A bastion of pan-Arabism was the Ba'ath Party, originally formed in Syria. The party's name means 'renaissance'. A party merger in 1952 had made it the Arab Ba'ath Socialist Party. The Ba'athists in Iraq lacked the Communists' numbers on the streets but were influential in the military. As it became clear that Qassem would keep Iraq out of any unification with other Arab states, the Ba'athists turned against him. In 1959, only one year after the revolution, they attempted an insurrection and tried to kill Qassem. Saddam Hussein, at age 23, was in the unsuccessful assassination team.

In 1963, the CIA backed a coup against Qassem because of his pro-Soviet policies. Ba'athists were prominent among the military faction that now came to power. Several days of severe fighting were followed by several months of arrests and executions of Qassem's supporters, especially the Communists. The same year, the Ba'ath Party adopted a programme of collective ownership of agriculture, central planning and a one-party state. Most Ba'athists in the army opposed this new radicalism. A new coup pushed the radical Ba'athists out of power in late 1963 and the army crushed the Ba'athist militia in street-fighting.

The catastrophic Arab defeat by Israel in 1967 inspired a distrust of military regimes that helped pave the way to the 1968 revolution in Iraq. This time Ba'athists acted in unity and alone. The President and Chairman of the Revolutionary Command Council (RCC) was Ahmad Hassan al-Bakr, once a member of the Free Officers. A close relative of his was Deputy Chairman of the RCC – Saddam Hussein, aged 31, with responsibility for internal security. All the influential players had military backgrounds except Saddam. Family and clan connections helped him get over that handicap; political skill and ruthlessness took him the rest of the way to the top.

Long before he became President, Saddam was described as the regime's 'strong man'. The label was well-earned in a regime that distinguished itself for not only the efficiency but also the refinements of its system of repression. It began with the public execution of 14 alleged conspirators in 1969, to which hundreds of thousands of people came to bear witness at the behest of the regime and, though it was not said openly, to become a little complicit. Like many other repressive regimes, Ba'athist Iraq maintained a momentum of discovering plots and putting the plotters on trial. People could disappear – for a time or permanently – for uttering the mildest doubts about the state of the country. Families sometimes only learned that a son or father had been executed when the authorities required them to pay the funeral costs. Others were imprisoned for years without trial. Torture was commonplace and extreme. And through the widespread system of informers, reaching into every part of social and working life, the regime ensured millions of ordinary people were complicit with repression; those who refused to help the authorities knew they put themselves and their families at risk.

The Ba'athist years constructed a new elite in Iraq, with Arab Sunnis receiving a disproportionate share of government posts. Among Sunnis, in the rise to higher levels, clan loyalties were critical; like both al-Bakr and Saddam many senior figures came from the area of Takrit. At the same time, leftist and nationalist ideology survived and guided aspects of government policy. There was considerable successful investment in health, education and in basic infrastructure, such as good transport and clean water. One side of the Ba'athist regime was repression, cruelty and denial of rights for Kurds and for Shi'a Muslims; the other side was that a significant part of the new oil wealth was spent on measures that would benefit ordinary people. Those among the Sunnis who did not challenge the regime did not fare badly.

In 1979 Saddam Hussein took control of the state. Al-Bakr was placed under house arrest and at least 500 senior party officials were executed, including one-third of the RCC. Those RCC members who were not denounced proved their loyalty by joining the firing squads; once again, the Iraqi system of repression sought complicity from those – in this case, members of the political elite – who were themselves at risk.

Saddam Hussein now set out on a course that brought one disaster after another. In 1980 he ordered the invasion of Iran, launching a war in which from 500,000 to 1,500,000 people died and which was economically ruinous. When it ended in 1988, its consequences became the prelude to the next war. Heavy borrowing had been necessary to finance the war, and Saddam began to argue that the debts should not be repaid, since Iraq had fought the war on behalf of all Arabs against the traditional Persian foe. Arab solidarity, he argued, required that Iraq be allowed off repayments, an argument that cut no ice with Kuwait, a major creditor, which pressed for repayment.

Saddam had other grievances against Kuwait (see page 94) and in the first half of 1990 made a series of speeches warning that he would take action if he did not receive satisfaction. It is impossible to know what Saddam would have done had he faced a strong reaction from other Arab states and external powers. But the fact that he did not face a clear negative reaction may have offered him some encouragement that he could get away with making a move against Kuwait.

At the end of the Iran-Iraq war, despite using chemical weapons against Iran and against the Kurds, Iraq had been seen by the USA as a factor for regional stability. The revolutionary nature of Iran, and in particular the experience of the embassy hostages in 1979–81 made Iraq seem moderate in US eyes. US economic assistance during the war meant that by 1988 the Iraqi economy was more closely linked to the West than at any time since the Qassem years. Up until mid-1990, the USA persuaded itself that, tough as he was, Saddam Hussein was a leader with whom they could do business.

The US administration therefore soft-pedalled its reactions to his speeches in the first half of 1990. They were not alone in doing so. It seemed nobody took Saddam Hussein at his word.

THE KURDS

The international system is not going to permit the formation of a unified Kurdish state, the dream of some Kurdish leaders. But it can fairly be said that Kurds are a group that benefited from the war in 2003 and subsequent occupation. They had an opportunity for a degree of autonomy, for respect for their culture, and perhaps for getting the benefit from the oil in their traditional homeland – all things that had previously been systematically denied them.

The Kurdish people are united by geography and a common history that is believed to go back more than two millennia and can certainly be dated to the time of the founding of Islam. But there appears to have been little, if any, common sense of Kurdish identity until the declining years of the Ottoman Empire. As that Empire was divided up in the wake of World War I, the formation of a state of Kurdistan was a promise that was made and then quickly lost *(see map page 27)*.

As the new states of Turkey and Iraq were being formed, Kurdish tribes continued a centuries-long tradition of rejecting subjugation. To suppress Kurdish identity, the new states utilized law, education, exhortation and force, and treated Kurdish people's rights with such raw contempt that they consistently fed new rounds of resistance. Any attempt to acknowledge Kurdish culture or even language was treated, especially in Turkey, as an act of dangerous political dissidence. For several decades, Turkish law denied that there was such a group of people as the Kurds and in the 1980s laws were passed to prevent both people and places from having Kurdish names.

The reason there is no single state of Kurdistan, however, is not only explained by the enormous odds faced by Kurdish nationalists. It also results from internal differences. Kurds are divided by many factors: by differences of dialect that, in some respects, are as significant as the differences between, say, English and German; by the difficulties of travel and communication in their mountainous region; by their tribal social structure and by ensuing political differences. These divisions and differences have inevitably weakened Kurdish uprisings against the central authorities of Iran, Iraq and Turkey.

Kurdish uprisings in Iraq from the 1920s until into the 1990s met armed opposition from Kurds, sometimes fighting in tribal Kurdish forces and sometimes in government units. And from 1960 until just before the US invasion of Iraq in 2003, Kurdish politics in Iraq was characterized by deep division between two leaders – Mullah Mustafa Barzani, followed by his son, and Jalal Talabani. Mullah Mustafa took over the Kurdish Democratic Party (KDP) from Talabani in 1963; in 1975 Talabani formed the rival Patriotic Union of Kurdistan (PUK). There was a sense of unity only in times of extreme danger, and usually only briefly.

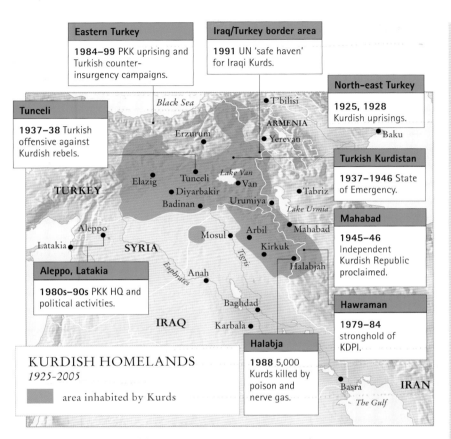

Eastern Turkey

1984–99 PKK uprising and Turkish counter-insurgency campaigns.

Iraq/Turkey border area

1991 UN 'safe haven' for Iraqi Kurds.

North-east Turkey

1925, 1928 Kurdish uprisings.

Tunceli

1937–38 Turkish offensive against Kurdish rebels.

Turkish Kurdistan

1937–1946 State of Emergency.

Mahabad

1945–46 Independent Kurdish Republic proclaimed.

Aleppo, Latakia

1980s–90s PKK HQ and political activities.

Hawraman

1979–84 stronghold of KDPI.

Halabja

1988 5,000 Kurds killed by poison and nerve gas.

Black Sea

T'bilisi

ARMENIA

Yerevan

Baku

Erzurum

Elazig · Tunceli · Van

Diyarbakir · Lake Van · Tabriz

Badinan · Urumiya · Lake Urmia

TURKEY

Aleppo

Latakia

SYRIA

Mosul · Arbil · Mahabad

Kirkuk

Halabjah

Euphrates · Tigris

Anah

Baghdad

IRAQ · Karbala

Basra · IRAN

The Gulf

KURDISH HOMELANDS
1925-2005

█ area inhabited by Kurds

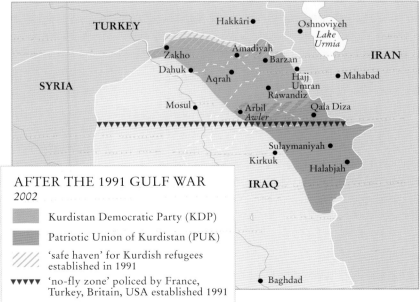

TURKEY

Hakkâri

Oshnoviyeh

Lake Urmia

IRAN

Zakho · Amadiyah

Dahuk · Barzan

SYRIA · Aqrah · Hajj Umran · Mahabad

Rawandiz

Mosul · Arbil · Qala Diza

Awler

Sulaymaniyah

Kirkuk

Halabjah

IRAQ

Baghdad

AFTER THE 1991 GULF WAR
2002

█ Kurdistan Democratic Party (KDP)

█ Patriotic Union of Kurdistan (PUK)

▨ 'safe haven' for Kurdish refugees established in 1991

▼▼▼▼ 'no-fly zone' policed by France, Turkey, Britain, USA established 1991

CHRONOLOGY *continued*

1975 Iran-Iraq agreement on Shatt al-Arab waterway. Iran ends support for KDP. In Iraq Patriotic Union of Kurdistan (PUK), led by Talabani, breaks away from KDP.

1978 Clashes between KDP and PUK leave many dead.

1979 KDP leader Mustafa Barzani dies – succeeded by son Massoud. Shah overthrown in Iran – KDPI seeks Kurdish autonomy. Fighting starts between government, KDPI and other Kurdish groups.

1980 Iraq invades Iran. KDP forces work with Iran, but PUK hostile to cooperation with Tehran.

1983 KDP and Iranian troops take Iraqi town of Hajj Umran. Iraqi troops kill 8,000 men from KDP leader's home area of Barzan. PUK and Iraq agree cease-fire.

1984 Kurdistan Workers' Party (PKK) launches guerrilla war in south-east Turkey from Syria. Iranian army defeats KDPI in Hawraman. Fighting starts between Kurdish groups.

1985 PUK/Iraq cease-fire fails.

1986 Iranian government sponsors reconciliation between KDP and PUK giving both its support.

1988 Iraqi 'Anfal Campaign' kills tens of thousands of Kurdish civilians and fighters. Hundreds of thousands exiled. One poison gas attack on Halabjah kills 5,000 Kurdish civilians.

1988 KDPI split on whether to negotiate with Iranian government.

1989 KDPI leaders shot dead when they arrive for secret talks with Iranian government in Vienna.

1991 March Kurdish uprising in northern Iraq. KDP and PUK joined by pro-government Kurdish militia units.

1991 March Iraqi forces rally from defeat by US-led coalition in Kuwait, suppress uprising in south then crush opposition in the north. 1.5 million Kurds flee, with hundreds of thousands trapped in mountains bordering Turkey.

April UN 'safe haven' on Iraqi side of border. PUK and KDP in talks with Iraq on Kurdistan autonomy.

1992 Iraqi Kurdish elections give KDP 50.8 percent of the vote and PUK 49.2 percent. Coalition government forms. 20,000 Turkish troops enter 'safe havens' in anti-PKK operation.

1994 Armed conflict starts between KDP and PUK in Iraqi Kurdistan.

1995 Turkish troops attack PKK in northern Iraq aided by KDP.

1996 KDP fights with Iraqi government against PUK. Rival PUK and KDP governments both claim sovereignty in Iraqi Kurdistan.

1998 KDP-PUK peace agreement – rival governments remain.

1999 Syria expels PKK. PKK leader Abdullah Ocalan captured. Death sentence commuted to life imprisonment. PKK cease-fire.

2003 On the eve of US offensive against Iraq PUK and KDP create joint leadership in the north. Turkish constitution amended to permit use of Kurdish language.

2004 PKK claims attacks by Turkish forces on Kurds in south-east Turkey, ends cease-fire. Turkish state television broadcasts first Kurdish language programme.

2004–05 Turkish government accuses PKK of bomb attacks.

2005 Alliance of Kurdish parties comes second in Iraqi national election – PUK leader Talabani elected interim President. KDP's Massoud Barzani is President of Kurdish autonomous region.

2006 Iranian and Turkish forces shell Kurdish targets inside Iraq.

2007 Turkish air raids on PKK targets in Iraq.

By the 1990s, there was open warfare between the KDP and the PUK. The KDP even allied with the Iraqi government of Saddam Hussein against the PUK. Likewise, the KDP assisted Turkish troops making forays into northern Iraq to root out forces of the Kurdistan Workers Party (known usually by its Turkish initials of PKK), which had been at war with the Turkish government since 1984.

The PKK is a leftist as well as nationalist party. It set out to gain strength both through political support from ordinary people and through terror tactics, which were directed both at the Turkish government and at Kurds who worked with it, as well as against rich Kurdish landowners.

Because of antagonism between Syria and Turkey, the PKK was able to have its headquarters in Syria, but security measures along that border meant they also needed bases in northern Iraq. When Syria turned against the PKK in 1998 and forced its leader Abdullah Ocalan to leave the country, a train of events was set in motion that ended early in 1999 with Ocalan being seized by Turkish agents as he was leaving the Greek Embassy in Nairobi, Kenya, where he had taken temporary refuge. His trial and life imprisonment (commuted from the death sentence which had long been unused in Turkey) created a moment of opportunity for the Turkish government to take a new course with the Kurds. With the incentive of future membership of the European Union, Turkey from 2002 set out to liberalize its constitution and laws to allow, among other liberties, greater rights for Kurds. The path of liberalization is not smooth, for the attempt to suppress Kurdish identity had become a deeply ingrained reflex in some parts of the Turkish state. Both in the judiciary and in the military as well as among some political opinion, the reasons for permitting diversity have yet to be fully understood and embraced. Nonetheless, some progress was registered though the recurrence of PKK violence from 2004 threatened the durability of these gains.

In 1991, in the immediate aftermath of that year's Gulf War, the USA encouraged Kurdish leaders in Iraq to rise up against Saddam. It then denied them direct assistance. The US calculation seems to have been that Saddam would be overthrown by a military coup when it was clear how much his power had been weakened. In fact, the US decision not to participate directly in overthrowing him, while respecting international law, simply played into his hands. His forces regrouped after defeat in the war, crushed the Shi'a uprising in southern Iraq, and then turned their attentions northwards. About one and a half million Kurds fled from the Iraqi advance. But in Turkey they were unwelcome refugees, because of the impact their presence could have had on political stability in the south-east. The creation of a 'safe haven' on the Iraqi side of the border was a path-breaking act by the UN, as the Security Council decided that barbaric behaviour by sovereign states within their own borders was an international concern. Many commentators interpreted the decision as the groundwork for a new era of international law and concern for human security. The US and British war on Iraq in 2003, by contrast, was widely seen as signalling an end to a short-lived era of respect for international law. Paradoxically, the Kurds of Iraq were again beneficiaries.

For the gains to be durable, however, several conditions had to be met. Kurdish political leaders would have to avoid the strategic shortcomings and internal divisiveness that ensue from clan loyalties. They would need to compromise with the leaders of the Arab Shi'a majority in Iraq on the form of governance, and come to a mutually acceptable deal on oil revenues. And they needed to find a way to assuage Turkish concerns that greater freedom and autonomy for Kurds in Iraq would be a model for Turkish Kurds and threaten the unity of the Turkish state.

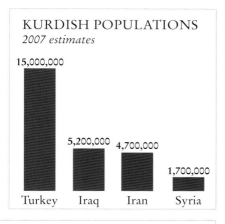

KURDISH POPULATIONS
2007 estimates

- Turkey 15,000,000
- Iraq 5,200,000
- Iran 4,700,000
- Syria 1,700,000

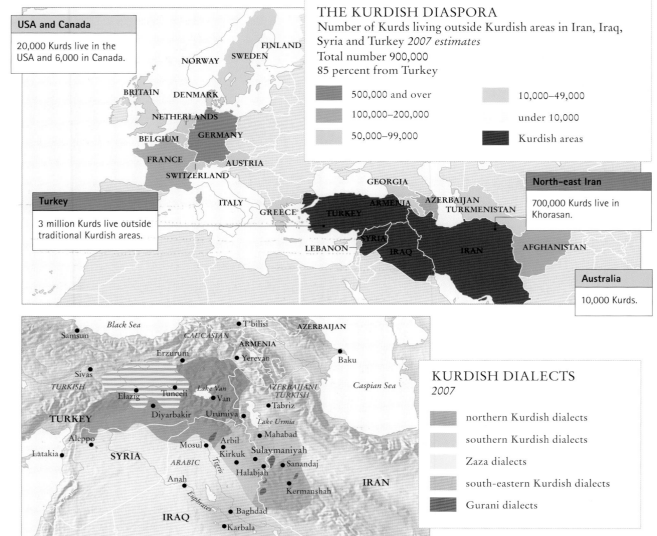

USA and Canada
20,000 Kurds live in the USA and 6,000 in Canada.

THE KURDISH DIASPORA
Number of Kurds living outside Kurdish areas in Iran, Iraq, Syria and Turkey *2007 estimates*
Total number 900,000
85 percent from Turkey

- 500,000 and over
- 100,000–200,000
- 50,000–99,000
- 10,000–49,000
- under 10,000
- Kurdish areas

North-east Iran
700,000 Kurds live in Khorasan.

Turkey
3 million Kurds live outside traditional Kurdish areas.

Australia
10,000 Kurds.

KURDISH DIALECTS
2007

- northern Kurdish dialects
- southern Kurdish dialects
- Zaza dialects
- south-eastern Kurdish dialects
- Gurani dialects

THE GULF WARS

At the end of the war with Iran in 1988, Iraq was weakened economically and had paid a heavy human price for starting the war in 1980, yet had a relatively strong international political position. Its key advantages included, first, its enormous oil reserves with which it was in a good position to repair in time the economic damage. Second, despite their losses, Iraq's armed forces were the strongest in the Gulf region and were regarded with respect by Western strategic commentators. And third, because Iran was treated with so much suspicion as a revolutionary regime, Iraq had received significant support from the West, especially the USA, during the war and had the possibility of continuing to benefit from these good relations.

Over the next 15 years, Saddam Hussein's regime lost all these advantages and finally lost power. US and British military intervention and occupation in 2003 were key elements in finally tipping the country into chaos and violence, but the foundations for disaster were laid by Saddam Hussein himself.

The war with Iran left Iraq heavily in debt, and in particular with a $14 billion debt to Kuwait. It was Saddam Hussein's position that Iraq had fought the war as defender of the Arabs against the traditional Persian enemy – not that this had actually featured in his strategic calculations when his forces attacked Iran in 1980. Accordingly, he claimed that the debt should be waived or eased. But by 1990, Kuwait was pressing for repayment. In OPEC, Iraq argued for overall cuts in production with a larger production quota for itself, so that oil prices and its own revenue would rise, permitting some debt repayment and funds for reconstruction. Iraq accused Kuwait of itself increasing production, in breach of its own quota, to keep oil prices down. Further, Iraq began to accuse Kuwait of slant drilling into neighbouring Iraqi oil fields – stealing Iraq's oil.

Almost all Iraq's port facilities had been destroyed during the war and there is little doubt that the additional coastline Iraq would gain by controlling Kuwait, together with its modern port, would offer Iraq improved long-term security. With this combination of elements, it was clearly tempting for Saddam Hussein to resurrect earlier territorial claims Iraq had made on Kuwait before its independence.

Despite Iraq's long list of loudly voiced grievances against Kuwait, the invasion in August 1990 – claimed at the time to be supporting a popular revolution in Kuwait, though no such revolution was under way – genuinely surprised other Arab states and the West. Reaction was quick, with both the Arab League and the UN condemning the invasion. Within a week, US forces started to deploy to Saudi Arabia to ensure Iraq would not make an even more ambitious military move, though there was no clear evidence that this was the intention.

A major diplomatic effort led by the Bush (Snr) administration in the

USA and supported by its western European allies and the Arab monarchies in the Gulf put together a 34-country coalition to enforce the UN demand for Iraq to quit Kuwait, with the legal backing of UN Security Council resolutions. When Saddam Hussein refused to pull his forces back, a one-month air offensive and a week-long ground war inflicted a decisive defeat and forced Iraq out of Kuwait. The speed and ease of the victory were another surprise. The USA discussed going further and taking the war into Iraq and all the way to Baghdad, but decided against exceeding the mandate from the UN.

There are no firm data on war deaths in Iraq resulting from the US-led offensive. Generally accepted estimates for military deaths are in the region of 10,000 during the air offensive and 10,000 during the ground war, while the civilian death toll is usually put at 2,500 – 3,500.

UN SECURITY COUNCIL RESOLUTIONS ON IRAQ- KUWAIT CRISIS 1990–91

2 August 1990 Resolution 660 Condemns invasion of Kuwait and urges Iraqi withdrawal.

6 August 1990 Resolution 661 Imposes economic sanctions against Iraq.

9 August 1990 Resolution 662 Declares Iraq's annexation of Kuwait 'null and void'.

25 August 1990 Resolution 665 Imposes a shipping blockade.

29 November 1990 Resolution 678 Authorizes use of 'all necessary means' if Iraq fails to withdraw by 15 January 1991.

3 April 1991 Resolution 687 Establishes cease-fire and requires Iraqi disposal of WMD.

US-LED COALITION FORCES IN THE 1991 GULF WAR
Contributing states
1990–91

other 10,000
of which:
Saudi Arabia 40,000
Egypt 35,000
Syria 20,000
Kuwait 7,000
Bahrain 3,000
Morocco 2,000

Arab states 107,000

USA 540,000

Britain 45,000

MAIN COALITION FORCES
Numbers of military personnel
1991

95

UPRISING AND VERIFICATION

In February 1991, the US administration decided not to advance to Baghdad and overthrow Saddam Hussein. There were several reasons why not: doing so was not authorized by UN resolutions, the coalition would have fallen apart, and the USA would then have had to run Iraq, which it did not want to do. President Bush (Snr) urged Iraqis to take matters into their own hands.

There were two uprisings: by Shi'a groups in the south and by Kurds in the north. The US coalition gave no direct assistance to either – except humanitarian aid in the north when the uprising was quashed. In the north, the USA, Britain and France imposed a no-fly zone but helicopters were exempt. The southern no-fly zone was not imposed until 2002. The US administration, anxious about the influence of the Iranian government on its co-religionist movements in southern Iraq, restricted support there even more than in the north. The consequences of the uprising's failure in the south were massacres, large-scale arrests and a programme to drain the southern marshlands to make the area easier to control. Saddam Hussein's regime emerged with its internal grip intact, despite defeat in Kuwait and the ensuing international isolation.

The UN Special Commission (UNSCOM) was established to monitor Iraq's biological, chemical and long-range missile disarmament, while the International Atomic Energy Agency (IAEA) focused on nuclear disarmament. Economic sanctions, imposed when Iraq invaded Kuwait in August 1990, were left in place after the war; in the UN resolution establishing the cease-fire at the end of the war, the prospect of removing the sanctions was made dependent on Iraq's abandonment of weapons of mass destruction (WMD) and the capacity to make them.

During 1991, nuclear bomb material was removed from Iraq and, by the end of 1992, most facilities used in Iraq's nuclear programme had been destroyed. The IAEA saw no discrepancies that gave grounds for believing that Iraq still had any nuclear capability, though total certainty is impossible when trying to prove a negative in a large country where information is so tightly controlled.

UNSCOM inspectors faced constant harassment from Iraq. They identified and eliminated 40,000 munitions for chemical weapons, 3,000 tonnes of chemical warfare agents and the ingredients for making them, and dismantled weapons programme facilities. In 1995, two sons-in-law of Saddam Hussein defected, telling UNSCOM that Iraq had carried out both chemical and biological disarmament in 1991. Iraq then gave UNSCOM a major archive on the WMD programme. In 1996, the defectors were enticed back to Iraq and assassinated by the regime.

Iraq never cooperated smoothly with UNSCOM and the IAEA. This has most often been explained in terms of Saddam's need to maintain not only control but also the appearance of, by not bowing down to the USA and its allies. It is also likely that he simply did not believe that he would gain anything by cooperating. Shortly after the war ended in 1991, both the British and US governments said that economic sanctions would remain as long as Saddam was in power, even though that was not stated in the UN resolution. If what later became known as regime change was already the goal of the USA and its closest ally in 1991, Saddam would have gained nothing by disarming.

Moreover, the Iraqi authorities were well aware that UNSCOM worked with Western intelligence agencies. This was neither wrong nor surprising. Providing intelligence information for UNSCOM inspectors to check was exactly what UN member states were supposed to do. But there is some evidence that the CIA tried to use UNSCOM as a cover for other activities. US cooperation with UNSCOM was fitful because news that Iraqi WMD could not be found, probably because there were none left, was politically unwelcome. In December 1998, all cooperation between UNSCOM and Iraq came to an end. The USA and Britain responded with attacks on suspected weapons facilities.

Economic sanctions, meanwhile, were hurting the ordinary people of Iraq. Independent studies suggest that sanctions to the end of 2000 led to approximately 350,000 deaths of children under the age of five. Some of these deaths can be traced also to the after-effects of the war and its destruction of basic infrastructure, including clean water supplies.

By insisting on keeping the sanctions going until Saddam was out of power, the USA and Britain and their supporters were effectively making the Iraqi people pay for the actions of their leader, over whom they had no control or influence, and by whom they were repressed and beaten down. Both the moral and the political logic of this were hard to fathom.

Under the pressure of public opinion to alleviate the misery, the UN instituted an oil-for-food programme in 1995: Iraqi oil would be sold and the income used for humanitarian need, war reparations, and for paying the costs of UNSCOM. $46 billion worth of humanitarian aid had been provided by the programme by the time it was closed down just before the 2003 war started. This eased the situation, but the sanctions still hurt. Worse, the programme became mired in scandal, with commission fees involving senior UN staff and over $4 billion being chanelled into the Iraqi regime's bank accounts. Oil smuggling produced a further $5.7 billion of illegal income for Iraq.

After the decisive moment of the 1991 war, Western policy on Iraq was inconsistent. A decade later, Saddam Hussein remained in power and one of the USA's regional problems remained unsolved. But everything changed radically with the US response to the September 2001 al-Qaida attack on the World Trade Center and the Pentagon.

UN SECURITY COUNCIL RESOLUTIONS 1991–2002

3 April 1991 Resolution 687 Establishes cease-fire and requires Iraqi disposal of WMD.

15 August 1991 Resolution 707 Urges Iraq to comply with the terms of Resolution 687.

12 June 1996 Resolution 1060 Ditto

21 June 1997 Resolution 1115 Ditto

23 October 1997 Resolution 1134 Ditto

12 November 1997 Resolution 1137 Ditto

2 March 1998 Resolution 1154 Warns of severe consequences of non-compliance with Resolution 687.

9 September 1998 Resolution 1194 Urges Iraq to comply with 687.

17 December 1999 Resolution 1284 UN Monitoring & Verification Mission (UNMOVIC) founded to replace UNSCOM.

8 November 2002 Resolution 1441 Declares Iraq in breach of 687 and requires Iraq's accurate accounting of WMD in 30 days, with serious consequences for non-compliance.

NO-FLY ZONES IN IRAQ
1992–2003

US and British air attacks

December 1992: Target Mig-25 aircraft. **Rationale** Iraqi incursion into no-fly zone.
January 1993: Target Radar and surface-to-air missile sites. **Rationale** Iraqi attacks, radar lock-ons. **Target** Nuclear research facility. **Rationale** Non-cooperation with UNSCOM.
June 1993: Target Intelligence HQ, Baghdad. **Rationale** Assassination attempt on ex-President Bush.
April 1994: Target Various military targets. **Rationale** Iraqi radar lock-ons.
December 1998: Target Biological, chemical and nuclear facilities. **Rationale** Non-cooperation with UNSCOM. **Target** Air defence battery. **Rationale** Radar lock-ons.
April 2002–03: Target Various military targets. **Rationale** General threat from Iraqi terrorism/WMD.

WAR 2003

The war fought against Iraq by the USA and Britain in 2003, with small contingents from Australia and Poland, was swift and efficiently won. More ambitious in scope than in 1991, it took a little less time and its death toll was not much greater.

The overthrow of Saddam Hussein had not been a US war aim in 1991, but became so afterwards, and there was a US-backed coup attempt in 1996 that went badly wrong. In 1998, an influential group wrote publicly to the Clinton administration urging it to remove Saddam. Among them was Donald Rumsfeld, appointed Secretary for Defense in 2001. In the build-up to the 2003 war he continued to identify regime change as US policy, but in the international debate in 2002, the emphasis fell on the problem of Iraq's weapons of mass destruction (WMD). The suicide attacks on the World Trade Center in New York and the Pentagon on 11 September, 2001 were so spectacular that the WMD issue got a new dimension – the possibility of terrorists such as al-Qaida getting WMD from a source such as Iraq.

Tales of links between al-Qaida and Iraq, however, never seemed even slightly credible. Osama bin-Laden, the leader of al-Qaida and long-range architect of the 9/11 attacks, had in 1990 proposed to the rulers of Saudi Arabia that a purely Muslim force be organized to defend the kingdom against Saddam. This was motivated primarily by the urge to keep US forces out of the Arabian peninsula but it also suggests a distinct lack of love between the religiously inspired al-Qaida and the secular state of Iraq. Not surprisingly, in the build-up to war there was no hard evidence of links between Iraq and al-Qaida and the case that WMD might be handed to terrorists was never persuasively made. The link always looked more like the work of an opportunistic publicist, who knew how to fuse two enemies in the public imagination, rather than the work of a careful intelligence analyst.

There is little doubt that it was widely believed in Western intelligence circles that Iraq had active WMD programmes. Some evidence existed – most notably, items that UNSCOM had calculated Iraq had at some time had but which were not found during the inspections from 1991 to 1998 – and this evidence was spun into a narrative in which supposition and possibility came to be treated as fact. In assessing these arguments retrospectively, it should never be forgotten than Saddam Hussein had repeatedly used chemical warfare in fighting both Iran and the Kurds, and equally that Iraq had always been uncooperative with UNSCOM. It was, in fact, a major shock for many politicians and commentators to find out, when US inspectors later had the run of the country, that there were no WMD in Iraq of any kind. It turned out that UNSCOM had been successful.

The UN Security Council sent the new monitoring mission, UNMOVIC, into Iraq at the end of 2002, with threats of serious consequences if Iraq did not cooperate. Iraqi cooperation was grudging and slow. Given the suspicion about Iraq and WMD, it was logical to pressurize Iraq into accepting a new round of UN inspections. The US military build-up exerted that pressure. When the USA and Britain refused to accept the further logic of letting UNMOVIC get on with its work, most observers concluded they were never serious about the process and were using it only as a means to get international support for a war they had long since decided upon. The impatience of the Bush administration in particular with the UN was a striking feature of the build-up to war.

The price of this impatience was that the war was fought without the legitimacy that a UN resolution would have given, and without very much international support. Though the Bush administration talked of a 'coalition of the willing', the upshot was that not many states were willing to do very much. There was a marked contrast with the situation in the 1991 war.

The lack of legitimacy was no more than an inconvenience in the war itself. But after the war, the lack of legitimacy was a serious and practical problem. British doctrine for peace operations emphasizes that legitimacy and popular acceptance of the mission are fundamental components of success. By sacrificing legitimacy, the US administration got the war it wanted, and Britain backed it, but at the same time they took the first step towards losing the peace.

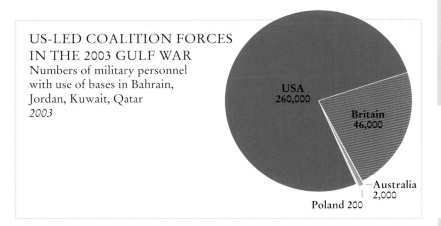

US-LED COALITION FORCES IN THE 2003 GULF WAR
Numbers of military personnel with use of bases in Bahrain, Jordan, Kuwait, Qatar
2003

USA 260,000
Britain 46,000
Australia 2,000
Poland 200

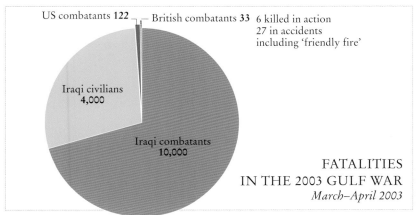

US combatants **122** — British combatants **33** 6 killed in action
27 in accidents
including 'friendly fire'

Iraqi civilians 4,000

Iraqi combatants 10,000

FATALITIES IN THE 2003 GULF WAR
March–April 2003

SIX WEEKS OF WAR

17 March President Bush ends diplomatic process giving Saddam Hussein 48 hours to leave Iraq.

19 March War begins with air and ground operations.

3–4 April US forces take Baghdad airport.

5 April US troops enter Baghdad.

7 April British forces take Basra.

9 April Baghdad falls – statue of Iraqi president pulled down.

10–11 April US and Kurdish troops take Kirkuk and Mosul.

14 April US forces take Takrit, Saddam's centre of power.

15 April Iraqi representatives attend a US-brokered meeting to set up Iraqi Governing Council.

1 May President Bush declares end of 'major combat operations'.

22 May UN Security Council Resolution 1483 ends sanctions against Iraq and provides mandate for US-led coalition presence.

December Saddam Hussein captured.

UN SECURITY COUNCIL RESOLUTIONS 2002–03

8 November 2002 Resolution 1441 Declares Iraq in breach of 687 and requires accurate Iraqi accounting of WMD in 30 days, with serious consequences for non-compliance.

22 May 2003 Resolution 1483 Lifts sanctions against Iraq and establishes mandate for the presence of USA and other international forces in Iraq.

OCCUPATION, INSURGENCY AND NEW GOVERNMENT

In May 2003, a memo by a senior British official described the office of General Garner, head of the Coalition Provisional Authority (CPA) as 'an unbelievable mess'. This judgement would soon be applicable to more than the state of the bureaucracy. Among other things, the US occupation forces have lost 190,000 weapons and the CPA lost $9 billion of oil revenue before it dissolved in June 2004. But the biggest chaos was in Iraq itself with a death toll that even by modest estimates was over 90,000, rampant crime, widespread insecurity – and about 1.8 million people having fled the country as refugees.

There were some gains. Five years after Saddam's overthrow there was an elected government, new police and security forces existed, British forces had all but left, and Kurds and Arab Shi'a could believe in a future in which their rights might be acknowledged. And in the second half of 2007 there were initial signs that the level of violence as measured by the civilian death toll was declining.

The chaos was partly the result of deliberate and shrewd disruption by insurgent groups. As well as general terror attacks to promote instability and disorder, they targeted water, oil and power, as well as police recruits, the occupying forces and Iraqis who worked with them, religious sites, and qualified professionals such as doctors and lawyers. When they needed to hide, they imposed themselves on towns and villages and got cooperation through fear. The insurgents included al-Qaida and associated groups as well as former Ba'athists with whom they shared little except loathing for the Americans, the government, the Kurds and the Shi'a. The insurgent groups had initially proliferated wildly – there may have been as many as 70 by late 2004 – but reorganized later into five main groups.

There were also well organized Shi'a militias. The largest were the Badr militia, linked to the main Shi'a political group in the south, and the

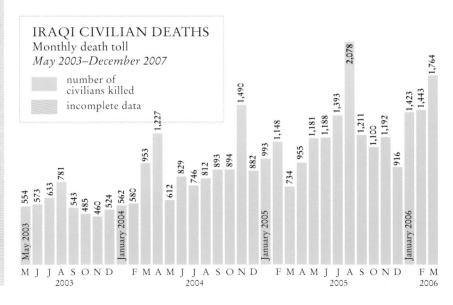

IRAQI CIVILIAN DEATHS
Monthly death toll
May 2003–December 2007

number of civilians killed

incomplete data

Mahdi Army led (though, reportedly, not always fully controlled or commanded) by the cleric Moqtada al-Sadr. Smaller groups were run by Shi'a politicians, and as they took hold of the levers of government many observers regarded the police as effectively a sectarian militia. The estimated strengths of these groups vary widely – from 10,000 to 50,000 for the Mahdi Army alone.

Facing this, the US Army routinely used massive force, as in its two assaults on Fallujah in 2004 that destroyed some 70 percent of the city. This is in line with the Soldier's Credo, which enjoins US soldiers not merely to defeat but to destroy the enemy. It works intimidatingly well in war but is less effective at winning the peace.

The 'surge' initiated by the USA in 2007 was partly about a relatively small increase in US force strength, and primarily entailed working with newly identified allies among armed groups in Iraq's towns and cities. By the end of 2007 the strategy appeared to be having some success as the death toll began to fall, though it was still almost twice as high as in May 2003 when occupation began.

Iraq's future depends on how efficiently and fairly the new state can function. The old state had always been regarded as unfair and unacceptable by the leaders of Iraq's largest communities, so power was based on fear. The civil war was triggered by the collapse of that state – a process begun by Saddam and completed by the USA. Five years on, nothing was settled about Iraq's chances for peace.

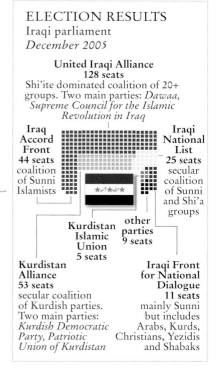

ELECTION RESULTS
Iraqi parliament
December 2005

**United Iraqi Alliance
128 seats**
Shi'ite dominated coalition of 20+ groups. Two main parties: *Dawaa, Supreme Council for the Islamic Revolution in Iraq*

**Iraq Accord Front
44 seats**
coalition of Sunni Islamists

**Iraqi National List
25 seats**
secular coalition of Sunni and Shi'a groups

**Kurdistan Islamic Union
5 seats**

**other parties
9 seats**

**Kurdistan Alliance
53 seats**
secular coalition of Kurdish parties. Two main parties: *Kurdish Democratic Party, Patriotic Union of Kurdistan*

**Iraqi Front for National Dialogue
11 seats**
mainly Sunni but includes Arabs, Kurds, Christians, Yezidis and Shabaks

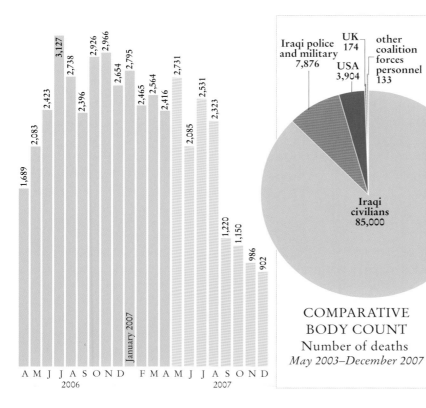

COMPARATIVE BODY COUNT
Number of deaths
May 2003–December 2007

Iraqi police and military 7,876

UK 174

USA 3,904

other coalition forces personnel 133

Iraqi civilians 85,000

Bar chart values: 1,689 | 2,083 | 2,423 | 3,127 | 2,738 | 2,396 | 2,926 | 2,966 | 2,654 | 2,795 | 2,465 | 2,564 | 2,416 | 2,731 | 2,085 | 2,531 | 2,323 | 1,220 | 1,150 | 986 | 902

January 2007

A M J J A S O N D   F M A M J J A S O N D
2006   2007

There is considerable controversy about how many civilians have been killed in Iraq since the end of the six-week war in 2003. Estimates go as high as a million, with one widely reported study producing a figure of 655,000 deaths by mid-2006, based on surveys of households in locations chosen as representative. These figures imply that in some months there have been almost 1,000 violent deaths per day, with nobody reporting or registering the fact. The figures shown here are from the organization Iraq Body Count, whose method is to count deaths reported by two separate media sources. On this reckoning the total civilian toll by the end of 2007 was about 85,000 deaths. It must be regarded as the minimum estimate.

SAUDI ARABIA

Saudi Arabia's crude oil reserves are about 22 percent of the world total, and its oil output is about 13 percent. The difference between those two figures means that Saudi Arabia's importance in the world oil industry will not soon diminish. What happens in Saudi Arabia, therefore, has a worldwide significance; disruption of supply or deliberate price hikes would damage Europe and, in particular, Japan, and via those economies have even wider effects. Such a wealth of natural resources and, with them, such a key place in the world economic system could destine a country, in principle, either to be a prize for others to compete over and take, or to be itself a key player on the world stage. It has taken considerable skill and determination for the Saudi monarchy to be the latter.

The Saudi system of rule owes much to both faith and tradition. The Saud family has espoused the puritanical Wahhabist form of Sunni Islam since the mid-18th century. Originally, Prince Saud provided Sheikh Wahhab with a vehicle for proselytizing, while Wahhabism, with its focus on cleansing the Islamic faith of distortions, became a source of moral and religious legitimacy for Prince Saud and his successors' rule. The Sauds briefly held Mecca and Medina in the early 19th century but were forced out by the Ottomans and punished. Through the 19th century, the Sauds competed for power in Arabia with two other great families – the Rasheeds and, for long the most powerful of the three, the Hashemites, descendants of the Prophet and guardians of the holy places of Mecca and Medina. It was an alliance with the British that eventually gave the Sauds the upper hand in warfare against first the Rasheeds and then, by the mid-1920s, against those other British allies, the Hashemites.

Ibn Saud founded the kingdom of Saudi Arabia on the basis of armed strength, monarchical rule and Wahhabism. Six years after the kingdom was established in 1932, oil was discovered. Revenues were modest until after World War II and in the 1950s they began to increase quickly. Oil money became a fourth pillar of Saudi power, both at home and, later, abroad. But oil money has also become a source of potential weakness.

With oil wealth have come allegations of gross extravagance by the royal family and scandals such as the al-Yamamah deal with British Aerospace in 1985. A decade later, media reports surfaced about a special fund connected to the deal, aimed at providing members and associates of the Saudi royal family with luxuries – travel, sports cars, yachts, cash for gambling – as sweeteners to ensure a follow-on contract. In 2004 it was alleged that over time this fund amounted to £60 million.

Even without corruption the availability of large sums of money makes it difficult for a monarchy whose legitimacy has a religious basis – both because of its Wahhabist roots and because of its role as guardian of the holy places – to maintain the necessary degree of purity in all its dealings.

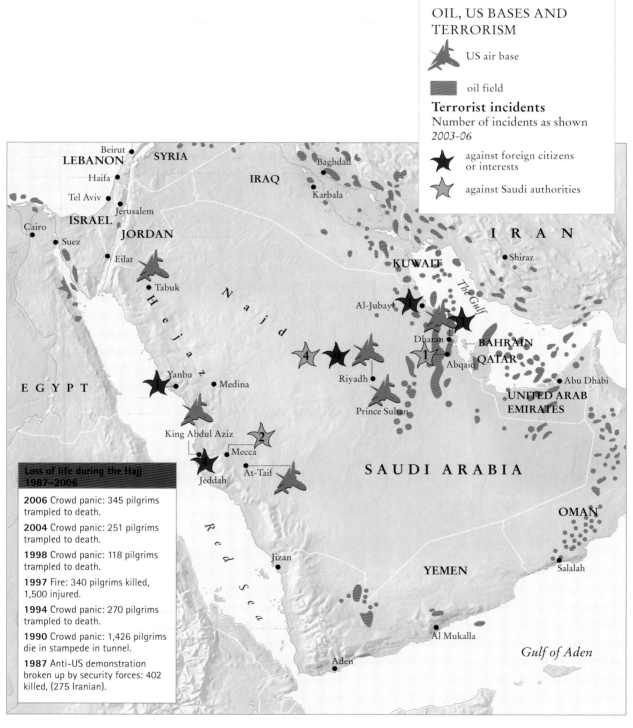

OIL, US BASES AND TERRORISM

US air base

oil field

Terrorist incidents
Number of incidents as shown
2003-06

against foreign citizens
or interests

against Saudi authorities

Loss of life during the Hajj 1987–2006

2006 Crowd panic: 345 pilgrims trampled to death.

2004 Crowd panic: 251 pilgrims trampled to death.

1998 Crowd panic: 118 pilgrims trampled to death.

1997 Fire: 340 pilgrims killed, 1,500 injured.

1994 Crowd panic: 270 pilgrims trampled to death.

1990 Crowd panic: 1,426 pilgrims die in stampede in tunnel.

1987 Anti-US demonstration broken up by security forces: 402 killed, (275 Iranian).

1986 'Custodian of the Two Holy Mosques' is added to King Fahd's official title.

1987 Iranian pilgrims riot during the *Hajj* in Mecca – 402 killed.

1989 Kuwaiti Shi'ites detonate several bombs during the *Hajj*. One person dies. Kuwaiti Shi'ite suspects caught and beheaded.

1990 Iraq invades Kuwait. King Fahd requests US troop presence.

1991 Saudi Arabia forces join war against Iraq in Kuwait.

1993 *Majlis* formed with 60 members.

1996 Truck bomb explodes at a US military apartment complex, killing 19.

1997 Number of *Majlis* members raised to 90.

1998 Saudi government bars use of Saudi airbases for attacks on Iraq.

2001 Saudi government bars use of airbases for attacks on Afghanistan; non-combat military flights are permitted. *Majlis* increases to 120.

2002 US permitted use of one airbase for defensive missions.

2003 May Suicide bombers kill 26 at Western housing compounds in Riyadh. **August** 90 percent of US military personnel withdrawn. **October** Unprecedented reform rally – 270 arrests. **November** *Majlis* gains right to propose legislation without prior royal permission.

2004 UK police open criminal investigation of British Aerospace scandal.

2005 King Fahd dies, succeeded by Crown prince Abdullah. Saudi Arabia joins WTO. *Majlis* increases to 150. First nationwide municipal election – women denied the vote.

2006 UK goverment ends criminal investigation into arms scandal on grounds of national security.

2007 US investigation of British Aerospace begins.

Beyond that, as the world oil price goes up and down, so does the state's income. The foundation-stone of the Saudi economy is thus inherently unstable – and the core of the most militant opposition that the monarchy faces is made up of those whose lives are both dislocated and coloured with disappointment by economic uncertainty.

The traditionalism of the monarchy is expressed, for example, in a legal code that continues to use not only capital punishment but flogging and amputation as forms of punishment. Although the Criminal Code was revised in 2002 to include the right to legal representation and a ban on torture, human rights monitors recorded continued violations. The monarchical tradition is flexible enough to permit the cautious introduction of a sounding board for the rulers, in the form of the *Majlis*, an appointed assembly first convened in 1993. And in 2005 came the first experiment with democracy, in the form of elections for municipal authorities. The experiment was strictly limited: only men voted.

Within Saudi Arabia, the monarchy is under pressure from both traditionalists and modernizers. Some groups claim to be more Wahhabist than the ruling family and accuse it of deviating from its Wahhabist roots. Other groups seek an easing of political restrictions. While modest legal and political reforms are a limited concession to the reformers and liberals, there have also been efforts to reduce the pressure from the other side: growing restrictions on the USA's use of its airbases culminated in 2003 with the departure of most US military personnel. Proselytizing for Wahhabism abroad and providing the resources for building mosques, libraries and religious schools have also contributed to the effort to maintain Wahhabist legitimacy at home. There is no other comparable source for new religious building for Muslims in many countries, so Wahhabism is increasingly influential in shaping Islam internationally. But the frequency of major tragedies on the annual pilgrimage to Mecca, the *Hajj*, is another challenge to the monarchy's legitimacy since it is accused of complacency and neglect of its duties.

The terrorist incidents that became more frequent in Saudi Arabia from 2003 onwards were, in part, outgrowths of frustrated demands for change. The incidents imply the possibility of the country becoming a major battleground, with the monarchy confronted by forces that are equally – albeit differently – religious in motivation. Neither al-Qaida nor other groups that might wish to confront the Saudi monarchy in this way have the strength to do so yet. And in the aftermath of the US occupation in Iraq, a major concern for Saudi leaders was the rise of Iran's power and influence in the region. This multiplied their difficulties in addressing the internal challenge and simultaneously raised the stakes. Should al-Qaida or related groups develop a real capacity to challenge the monarchy, the prospect would have profound regional and international implications.

Political groups in Saudi Arabia

Neo-Wahhabists

Neo-Wahhabists oppose all secular authority and criticize official Wahhabism as deviating from Islamic fundamentals. Appeal to young, recently urbanized, unemployed men, but include members of the educated Saudi elite. The London-based Movement for Islamic Reform, part of the Committee for the Defence of Legitimate Rights suppressed by the Saudi authorities in 1993, organized anti-government demonstrations in Jeddah in December 2004.

Shi'a Islamists

Around 10 percent of the population is Shi'ite. Historically marginalized: few Shi'ites hold government jobs and they cannot join the armed forces. The Iranian Revolution radicalized some of the Shi'a population and in the late 1980s Ayatollah Khomeini openly advocated the overthrow of the Saudi monarchy. Some Shi'a Islamists have allied with liberals and Sahwists since 2002.

Sahwist Reformers

The Sahwist *al-Sahwa al-Islamiyya* movement began in Saudi universities during the 1960s and 1970s, influenced by Muslim Brothers who found refuge in Saudi Arabia after persecution in Egypt and Syria. Socially conservative and with a clear Sunni identity, they support increased popular participation in politics and greater social justice. The Sahwists are the leading force in a coalition with Shi'a Islamists and Liberals.

Liberal Reformers

A diverse group, mainly of technocrats and businessmen. Some advocate a more flexible interpretation of Wahhabism while others are close to neo-Wahhabism in outlook. Allied with Sahwists since 2002.

Rejectionists

Rejectionists are Islamists who regard the notion of the state as illegitimate and whose focus on faith, rituals and morality takes them out of political participation. It was Rejectionists who took over the Grand Mosque in Mecca in 1979. Some have joined more militant groups.

al-Qaida

Groups of fighters mobilized for the Afghan War in the 1980s and opposed to US deployment in Saudi Arabia. al-Qaida challenged the legitimacy of the Saudi monarchy's claim to be guardian of the holy sites. Their direct links with Saudi Arabia were probably broken by a major security crackdown in 2003–04, but the group al-Qaida in the Arabian Peninsula (QAP) remained active and attacked Western targets in Saudi Arabia. A QAP offshoot, the Haramain Brigade concentrates its attacks on Saudi targets.

DANGER AND OPPORTUNITY

Of the factors that shaped today's Middle East – Islam, the Ottoman Empire, European colonialism, the foundation of the state of Israel, US power and oil – history has closed the book only on the Ottoman and European empires. Even so, their legacies remain important. The other four factors persist, joined by two more to shape current political dilemmas and opportunities – demography and the nature of governance.

These factors together create the potential for violent conflict. The opportunities for more widely shared prosperity, increased freedoms and peace are relatively few. That means something special is required to seize them; with business as usual, things will continue as they are or deteriorate.

DEMOGRAPHY

The population of the region is growing faster than its economy and is on average younger than in most European countries. If there is no strong and sustained acceleration of economic growth, resources and opportunities will be spread thinly. There is a serious risk of growing frustration and disaffection.

In the absence of economic improvement at home, some people will emigrate and meet Europe's need to expand its productive labour force. Most will not, however, and of them, many will remain frustrated in their hopes and ambitions for rewarding lives. In today's Middle East, it is alienation and frustration that, as much as any other factors, perpetuate the risks of violent conflict by creating pools of recruits for social and political causes and, at the extreme, for armed groups.

In principle, two things could answer the challenge. The first is that these problems are by no means necessary consequences of a growing population. A relatively young population can be dynamic and creative, a source of opportunity for economic growth, new ideas, and reform. And then there is oil.

OIL

Oil provides the basis for economic growth. Oil resources are spread unevenly so that some countries benefit disproportionately, but economic growth in one country tends to benefit its neighbours. In the Middle East, where a common language and similar customs facilitate labour mobility and trade, it ought to be straightforward for oil-based economic growth to provide general regional benefit.

Judging by past and current performance, this expectation will not be met. In most countries oil wealth will probably not liberate the economic energies of relatively young populations, but will instead act as a palliative – a way for the ruling group to avoid facing up to real problems that confront them.

A tanker takes on oil from the Mini-Al Basrah offshore terminal.

Middle Eastern oil is set to be an important factor in the global economy for decades ahead unless demand drops. There are three ways that might happen: alternative sources of oil, conservation and non-oil sources of energy. There are modest prospects for conservation and alternative energy sources, thanks to anxiety about the environmental effects of continuing to rely on fossil fuels. And there are some prospects of new oil sources, not least in sub-Saharan Africa. However, China and India will provide comfortably enough demand to match supply as they continue to grow towards their anticipated positions as the world's largest and third largest economies respectively by 2020.

A great wealth of natural resources allows a ruling elite to avoid making the kind of sacrifices – or at least, moderation of its appetites – that are required for legitimacy among the people. Historically, the need to get taxes approved is one big reason why undemocratic forms of government had to become democratic. When a government can finance itself from oil and buy off troublemakers without taxation, it may calculate it has not much need for the active consent of the governed.

Clock with Hebrew characters on Ottoman tower in the old city of Acre.

GOVERNANCE

Throughout the region, deficiencies in democracy and respect for human rights are all too evident. In many countries, these deficiencies go along with corruption, inefficiency, extravagance, incompetence and favouritism.

In the Middle East, with the obvious exception of Israel, virtually all governments refer to Islam for legitimacy. The difficulty is that Islam is very demanding about how the faithful should be governed. It generates standards that, if not formally democratic, nonetheless derive from respect for the worth and dignity of individuals and from a deep sense of fairness – values that are themselves at the heart of democracy at its best. These values lead, for example, to cherishing the idea that the leader should live in a modest style, as ordinary people do, an ideal embodied in the life of the Prophet. When and where government is corrupt, extravagant, blind to the welfare of the people and oppressive, it risks a religious rejection of the government's claim to legitimacy. By claiming a legitimacy based on faith, governments risk facing religiously inspired opposition.

Ruling groups' strategies for dealing with the dilemma fall into two categories. They can maintain themselves by stasis, as with the monarchies or Egypt and Algeria during the civil war, conceding as little reform as possible. But by blunting reform, they risk revolution. Other governments keep their balance by permanent forward momentum – Iran, Iraq under Saddam Hussein, Libya and Syria. They take one risk after another in confrontations with enemies at home and abroad, because they will not survive by opting for a quiet life.

Olive tree, Jerusalem.

ISLAMISM

Against this background, movements and parties that express their political programmes in terms of religious renewal are attractive. They offer a clean alternative that attends to the welfare of the people. Many derive their legitimacy as much from the practical and material good they do as from their emphasis on faith or the militancy with which they oppose US power and Israel.

The Islamists are forceful as an opposition but have had little chance to be tested in government. Where they have, the signs are not good. In the very different cases of Iran and, outside the region, Sudan and Afghanistan under the Taliban, peace and increasing freedom have not been valued highly. Nor are they good examples of economic efficiency. The appalling violence that Islamist groups were prepared to use during the Algerian civil war has also been treated by many observers as an illustration of the dangers of Islamism. Despite accusations from some quarters that Hamas, which controls Gaza and participated briefly in the Palestine Authority coalition government in 2006-07, fell into familiar corrupt ways as soon as it tasted power, the jury is still out on its ability to retain integrity in power; there is less disagreement that it exerts power arbitrarily.

There is great diversity among those who seek political inspiration from faith in Islam. The Wahhabist monarchy of Saudi Arabia and the Shi'a religious leaders of Iran have profound political disagreements and diverge from each other on social and economic issues too. More broadly, there is debate within Islamist movements about whether state power is the right goal to aim for, as well as about democracy, social diversity, the role of women and education, and how to interpret the Quran. And while most Islamists accept the reality of existing states and their borders, a more radical minority seeks to overthrow the whole system and establish a Caliphate across the whole region.

These diverse strands of opinion are unified by anything seen as an attack on Islam, exemplified by the way cartoons in an obscure Danish magazine in 2005 stoked fury and riots in some Arab countries.

This anger feeds on a sense of injustice. Part of it is focused on the USA, and the old colonial powers – especially Britain – remain in the picture for their historical role and for not completely abandoning it. But the main long-term focus for Muslim anger is Israel – its existence, the illegal actions it seems to get away with, and the injustice suffered by Palestinians. Arguments that Europe and North America have sustained Israel's legitimacy are based on centuries of crimes against Jews in Europe culminating in the Holocaust. Many in the Middle East regard these horrors as not their business. The crimes happened elsewhere, yet somehow the region is forced to pay for them.

ISRAEL

Seen from Israel, the issue is security. Seen from Palestine, and generally in the region, the issue is justice. By the time Israeli forces moved into the West Bank in 2001 in the second *intifada*, Israel no longer regarded negotiations with the Palestine Authority as worthwhile. With the election of Hamas in early 2006, Israel entrenched its rejection of negotiation. But could Israel achieve security by imposing an arrangement for Gaza and the West Bank of its own choosing?

The unilateral approach could work if three conditions were fulfilled. First, Israel needed support from the USA and other powers outside the region; this seemed likely. Second, Israel needed tacit acceptance from Middle Eastern governments so they would not support attacks on Israel. This seemed possible for several governments, but could never be granted by some, such as Iran and Syria, and would be too great a risk for some other governments struggling for legitimacy. And third, Israel needed Palestinian acquiescence, which was implausible except in the most limited, sullen and potentially explosive form.

Beyond this, Israel does not exist in a security vacuum. In Iraq, some of the insurgent groups hate Israel more than the USA, are not exclusively concerned about Iraq, and have become stronger and more deadly through combat experience. The absence of a mutually accepted settlement with the Palestine Authority risks bringing more radical groups into the picture.

So, the balance of probability was against Israel achieving peace unilaterally. A peace initiative launched in late 2007 excluded Hamas, and in early 2008 the inevitable result was an escalation in violence mainly in the form of missile attacks. And the likely consequences will be felt not only in Israel and the Occupied Territories, but also more widely.

Israel plays a particular role in the politics of other Middle Eastern countries. It is used by governments to explain why their development policies have not worked, while opposition groups use it to berate governments for not having done enough against Israel. Either way, Israel provides a distraction from internal social and economic development problems, and will continue to until there is a settlement that Palestinians perceive to be just.

The nuclear weapon issue is connected to this. Nuclear weapons will not make any Middle Eastern state safer, but the fact that Israel has them offers a justification that is widely accepted in the region for others to do likewise. International concern about the issue focused on Iraq for some years until their absence was discovered in 2003. By 2005, the spotlight had shifted to Iran. Its commitment to uranium enrichment was seen by Israel and the USA as evidence of nuclear weapon ambitions, which Iran denied.

Israeli security wall, Jerusalem.

THE USA

'I really do believe we will be greeted as liberators'

Vice President Dick Cheney, March 2003.

'We know that he [Saddam Hussein] has been absolutely devoted to trying to acquire nuclear weapons, and we believe that he has, in fact, reconstituted nuclear weapons.'

Vice President Dick Cheney, March 2003.

'I don't believe anyone that I know in the administration ever said that Iraq had nuclear weapons.'

Secretary of State Donald Rumsfeld, May 2003.

Since the 1950s, the US role in the region has grown in prominence and forcefulness and has become a key determinant of progress on questions of peace and war. If it gets its policy wrong, it will undermine prospects for security in the region and at home.

There was a worldwide sense of disbelief in 2005 and 2006 when the US administration openly contemplated forceful action against Iran if it did not acquiesce to UN pressure to stop enriching uranium. Whether the US administration was right or wrong that the Iranian government was enriching uranium in order to get weapons, it was not clear why US threats against Iran would be credible while US forces remained bogged down in Iraq.

Iraq did not work out the way the Bush administration expected. US forces were not regarded as liberators and neither WMD nor evidence of continuing development of WMD were found. Inevitably, the Bush administration argued strongly that intervention in Iraq was a success, as did the British government. Although the results are not uniformly disastrous for all Iraqis, regarding the occupation as a success begged a question about how failure might look.

Accounts of US decision making before and during the war and the occupation of Iraq suggest a system that is Byzantine in complexity, intermittently imperial in attitude, and afflicted by intense in-fighting. In 2006, US Secretary of State Condoleeza Rice acknowledged 'tactical errors, thousands of them, I'm sure' – later remarking that she had not counted and the term was metaphorical. The many flaws include failures of intelligence and diplomacy; an absence of planning for the post-war; incompetence in the occupation authorities; overkill by the armed forces and abuse of human rights in Abu Ghraib and elsewhere.

Beyond these specifics, however, trying to spread peace and democracy by armed force is a paradoxical undertaking that has succeeded only rarely. To attempt to do so with a military action not authorized by the UN indicates distaste for the constraints of law, adding a further layer of paradox when the aim is to replace arbitrary authority with government based on the rule of law. Even if Iraqi democracy is eventually functional and stable, the human price has been great. And as well as its own human losses and the economic costs paid not just by the USA and its allies but by the world economy, the USA has paid a price in lost moral authority and tarnished legitimacy in the region. In short, by occupying Iraq, the USA got into a trap where even success must involve some degree of failure.

As the USA entered the 2008 election, it faced a fork in the road, with the choice to be made by the incoming administration in 2009. In one direction lay the USA's own worst nightmare – caught in perpetual warfare in the region, sky-rocketing oil prices, military expenditure soaring, with the inevitable consequences of a growing national debt and a negative balance of payments, while the unpopularity of the war at home weakens US armed forces because people do not volunteer for

110

wars they do not believe in – with terrorist attacks on the US homeland and on increasingly disaffected allies. Some parts of this nightmare scenario were already happening in 2007-08. The other way lay disengagement, which may be almost equally unpalatable for US leaders. This would not mean cutting off entirely from political and commercial links with the region, merely that the USA would cease attempting to determine the region's fate.

However, how new the policy will likely be after the 2008 election should not be overestimated. The Bush administration has produced particular calamities, but no observer of half a century of US Middle Eastern policy up to the occupation of Iraq could think disengagement a very likely option.

Nor would it be an easy alternative to implement. There would be significant pressure against it from the USA's closest regional allies. It would require withdrawal from Iraq with a relatively stable and democratic government in place, but the prospect of a US withdrawal could temporarily increase instability and violence yet more.

The main gain of disengagement would be to reduce US exposure to risk and emphasize the importance of legitimacy in international policy.

PROSPECTS

There is nothing in the record of external intervention in the Middle East that gives great grounds for optimism about it as a viable route to peace, democracy and shared prosperity. Good governance is an essential condition for economic and social development but trying to impose it selectively and forcibly will not work.

Middle Eastern societies have mostly experienced profound difficulties in dealing with the challenges posed by Western modernity. That they have been under constant Western pressure in combined economic, military, political and cultural forms has made it hard for them to find their way. The failings of their leaders, ranging from short-term miscalculations to corruption and repression, have taken the limited opportunities that existed and wasted each one.

The prospects for peace are not comforting, but developments can be unexpectedly positive: it is worth recalling that Algeria managed to find its way out of a brutal war. Even in the Israel-Palestine conflict, dialogue is possible if leaders on both sides seek it, and they may see it as in their interests. For Israel and Hamas to negotiate, both would have to change their entrenched positions, but if they do not negotiate both may find themselves under attack from the real radicals in the region. For the USA, making its presence in the region less intrusive may be hard to swallow, but continuing to be as intrusive entails proven risks. In Iran, voices that counselled caution over uranium enrichment were heeded. The situation is precarious but everywhere there is opportunity as well as danger.

A young child makes her way through a garbage pit on the outskirts of Sadr City, Iraq, May 2006.

PART THREE   THE STATE OF THE NATIONS

The Middle East is a region of immense internal variety and diversity, though people from outside the area often lose sight of that. One reason for this is simply that what one sees from a distance is often somewhat indistinct and visible only in broad outline. Too often this can feed an essentially racist assumption that the differences between, for example, the region's ethnic groups do not matter. And this both feeds and is fed by fear about the threat to some of the world's richer countries coming from the Middle East – a fear that combines with misperception to lead inevitably on to ignoring the threat to the Middle East coming from some of the world's richer countries.

Another reason is very different: it is that in order to understand the Middle East, it is important to grasp two seemingly contradictory realities and appreciate that it is both a unified region and highly diverse at the same time. The Middle East is bound together through the various historical, religious, cultural, economic and political influences that have shaped it. Within that unity its diversity has been shaped by the self-same influences.

One way to view the world – or any region within it – is through statistics. These permit comparisons both within a region and with the rest of the world, and they are often a fruitful way of gaining insight into broad social, political and economic trends. Statistics, however, are notoriously capable of leading the observer astray.

Statistics are not facts but a way of representing facts. The very process of gathering the data smoothes out differences and masks diversity. Statistical comparison therefore involves a large amount of estimation. Data about the same issue from different sources are consequently often quite incompatible each other – sometimes for technical reasons and sometimes because of the political agendas or blinkers of the organizations presenting the data. Some important phenomena simply fall out of the statistics: when Iraq was internationally isolated after 1991, for example, it disappeared from some international data collection. Palestinians are also statistically invisible in some data collection as are other groups in the Middle East. Statistics have historically tended to ignore gender difference, though this is a problem that has been recognized and is steadily being resolved.

Overall statistics are useful – but only if they are treated with care by statisticians, researchers and readers alike.

People at peace,
Lebanon, 2000

ETHNICITY AND LANGUAGE

The population of the region is about 350 million people, of whom about two-thirds – approximately 240 million – are Arabs. The largest other population groups in the region are Persian, Berber (speaking Tamazight), Kurdish and Jewish. Persians form just over half of the population of Iran, and Jews are the majority in Israel, while there are large Berber populations in Algeria and Morocco, and significant numbers of Kurds in Iran, Iraq and Syria.

The most straightforward distinguishing feature of Arabs is the language. Arabic has been a written language since at least the 5th century CE, two centuries before the time of the Prophet, and spread through the region along with the spread of Islam as the language of the Quran. There is today a standard form of Arabic that is written, used for formal situations, and taught in schools. In vocabulary and grammar it is the same as the Arabic of the Quran. As well as the standard form, there are also a large number of regional versions used in daily speech. These colloquial forms of Arabic vary widely enough to be mutually incomprehensible in some cases. Educated Arabs tend to be conversant in both standard Arabic and their own colloquial form.

Because Arabic is the language of Islam, Iranian mullahs have also traditionally learned it, especially those who teach in the major religious centres.

The common formal language provides great potential advantages for regional cooperation in communication, university education and research, politics, trade and economic development.

LANGUAGE IN THE MIDDLE EAST
Main language group
2008 or latest available data

- Arabic
- Hebrew
- Persian

Significant minority language groups
2008 or latest available data

- Bedawi
- Kurdish
- Tamazight
- Turkish
- Arabic

ETHNICITY IN THE MIDDLE EAST
Pie charts on map show proportion of total population
2008 or latest available data

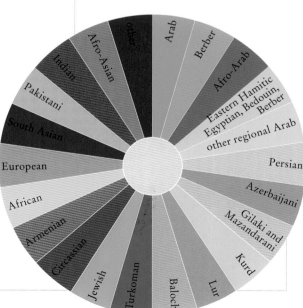

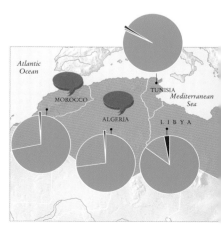

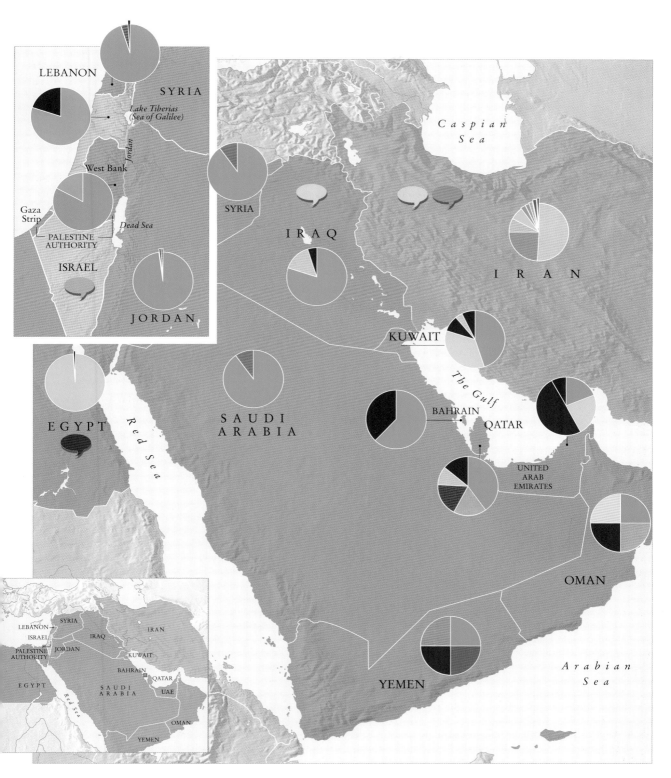

RELIGION

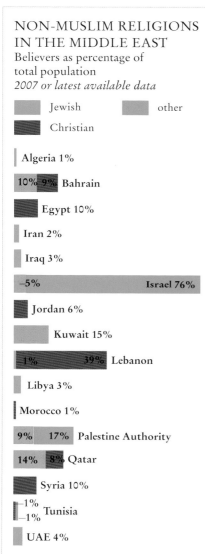

About 90 percent of the population in the Middle East are Muslims. However, Islam is far from a monolithic faith. The division between Shi'ites and Sunnis dates from the decades following the death of the Prophet in the 7th century CE. Though reliable statistics are not available, a credible estimate is that 65 percent of Muslims in the Middle East are Sunni and about 30 percent Shi'a. There are also divergences among the Shi'ites and there are other Muslim groups that distinguish themselves from both the two main forms.

Shi'ism is rather more structured in organization than Sunni Islam (though not as structured as most forms of Christianity). There are also different festivals and theological differences. The latter appear to be less numerous and significant than is the case in the cleavages in Christianity; Shi'ites and Sunnis recognize each other as Muslims and both groups adhere to the five pillars of the faith (belief in God and acceptance of Mohammed as Prophet; daily prayer; charitable giving; an annual fast; and going at least once on a pilgrimage to Mecca). The split between Shi'ites and Sunnis, though born in wars fought over who was the rightful successor to the Prophet, has also involved less violence than the century of bloodshed that accompanied the Reformation and Counter-Reformation in 16th- and 17th-century Europe.

The place of religion in Middle Eastern politics is imbued with a much deeper and wider significance because it is the birthplace of three world religions. The grip that Middle Eastern conflicts have on the attention of the rest of the world probably derives from religion as much as any other factor, if not more.

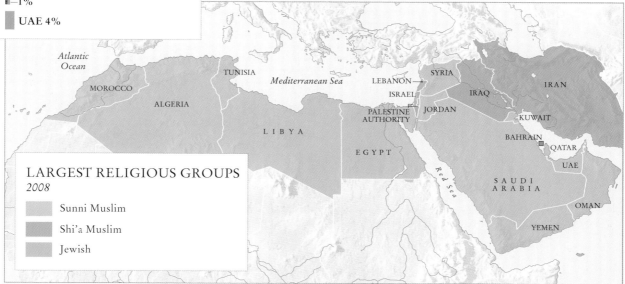

LARGEST RELIGIOUS GROUPS
2008

Sunni Muslim

Shi'a Muslim

Jewish

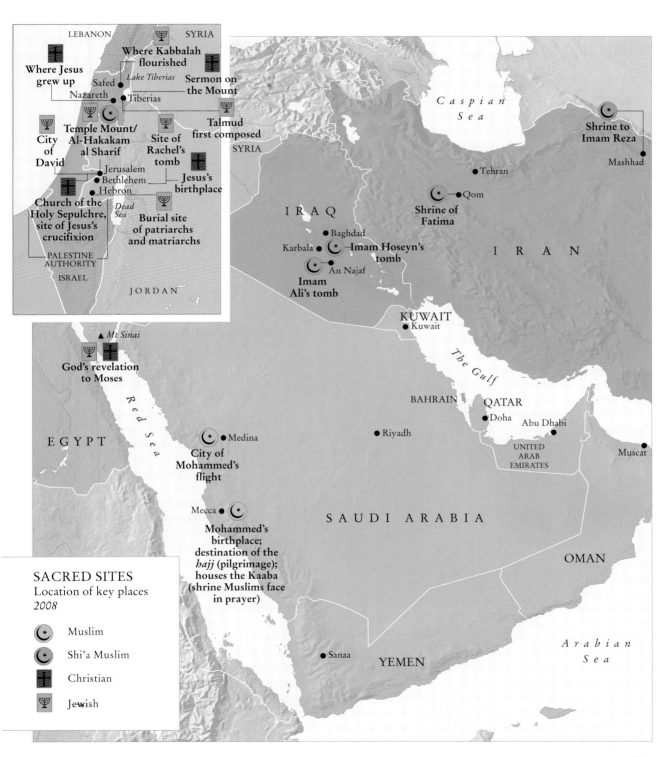

LEBANON SYRIA

Where Kabbalah flourished

Where Jesus grew up

Lake Tiberias

Sermon on the Mount

Safed
Nazareth
Tiberias

Temple Mount/ Al-Hakakam al Sharif

Talmud first composed

City of David

Site of Rachel's tomb

SYRIA

Jerusalem
Bethlehem
Hebron

Jesus's birthplace

Dead Sea

Church of the Holy Sepulchre, site of Jesus's crucifixion

Burial site of patriarchs and matriarchs

PALESTINE AUTHORITY

ISRAEL

JORDAN

Caspian Sea

Shrine to Imam Reza

Mashhad

Tehran

IRAQ

Qom

Shrine of Fatima

Baghdad

IRAN

Karbala

Imam Hoseyn's tomb

An Najaf

Imam Ali's tomb

KUWAIT
Kuwait

The Gulf

Mt Sinai

God's revelation to Moses

Red Sea

EGYPT

Medina

City of Mohammed's flight

BAHRAIN

QATAR
Doha

Abu Dhabi

UNITED ARAB EMIRATES

Riyadh

Muscat

Mecca

Mohammed's birthplace; destination of the *hajj* (pilgrimage); houses the Kaaba (shrine Muslims face in prayer)

SAUDI ARABIA

OMAN

SACRED SITES
Location of key places
2008

Muslim

Shi'a Muslim

Christian

Jewish

Sanaa

YEMEN

Arabian Sea

LIFE EXPECTANCY AND HEALTH

LIFE EXPECTANCY
AROUND THE WORLD
2005
selected regions

OECD countries	78.3
Latin America and Caribbean	72.8
East Asia and Pacific	71.7
Turkey	71.4
World average	68.1
Arab states	67.5
South Asia	63.8
Sub-Saharan Africa	49.6

The population of the Middle East is, by world standards, relatively young and growing quickly. The Middle East's population as a proportion of the global total has approximately doubled in the last half century, now standing at about five percent. Almost 40 percent of the region's population are under the age of 14 and only a little over five percent are over the age of 60.

Life expectancy is, however, increasing. Population trends indicate that a total regional population in the vicinity of 350 million people in the year 2000 will increase by approximately 150–200 million by the year 2020. The basic demographic data, such as life expectancy and the population's age structure, reflect the broad trends and condition of economic development.

The basic conditions of life vary widely, both from one country to another and between rich and poor within countries. Under-nutrition is a serious public health problem because many ailments that are minor matters for the well fed are potentially lethal for the under-nourished. Thus the proportion of underweight small children is indicative both of

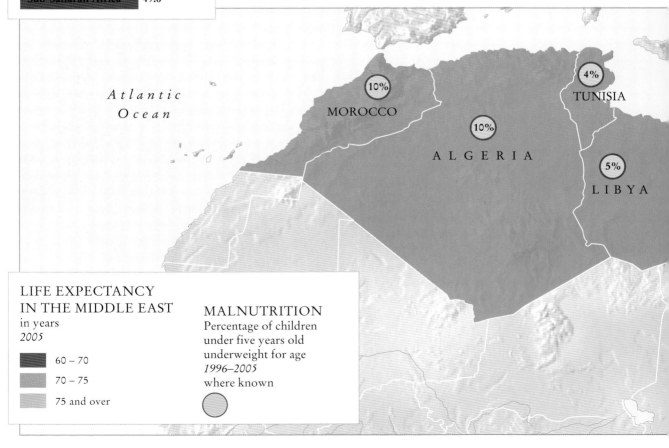

LIFE EXPECTANCY
IN THE MIDDLE EAST
in years
2005

- 60 – 70
- 70 – 75
- 75 and over

MALNUTRITION
Percentage of children
under five years old
underweight for age
1996–2005
where known

the overall state of health and of the degree of poverty.

The high incidence of malnutrition among the under fives in Yemen is a result of the overall lack of prosperity. The relatively high incidence in wealthier countries such as Oman, UAE and Saudi Arabia reveals the effect of social inequalities.

Though child malnutrition statistics are not available for Iraq, it became a serious problem in the 1990s and mortality among under-fives increased by 150% from 1990 to 2003. This was a consequence both of the 1990-91 war and of the economic sanctions that Iraq faced from then until the next war in 2003.

There was considerable controversy about how much suffering the sanctions caused. It has been estimated that, by the end of 2000, 350,000 children had died, with several hundred thousand more chronically malnourished. These estimates were vigorously challenged and as vigorously defended. Whatever the precise figures, malnutrition was virtually unknown in Iraq before the period of sanctions, when it became a major public health problem.

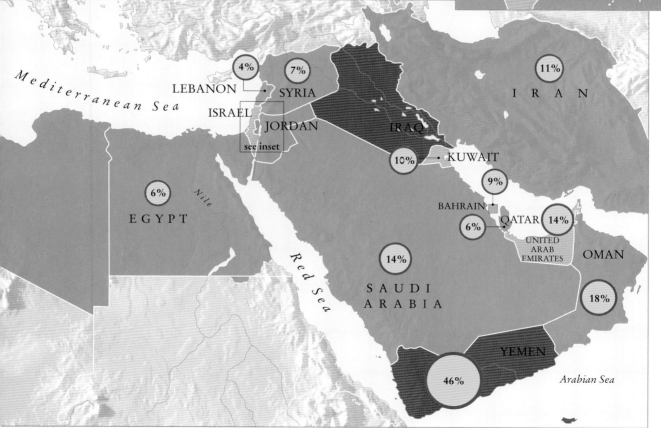

POPULATION AND URBANIZATION

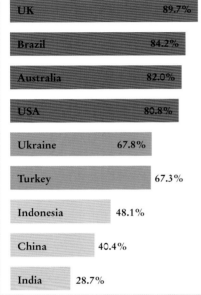

URBAN POPULATION AROUND THE WORLD
Percentage of total
2005

UK	89.7%
Brazil	84.2%
Australia	82.0%
USA	80.8%
Ukraine	67.8%
Turkey	67.3%
Indonesia	48.1%
China	40.4%
India	28.7%

S ome countries in the Middle East – Israel, Jordan, Lebanon, Libya, and several of the states of the Arabian peninsula – are as urbanized as the USA. Others – such as Algeria, Egypt, Iran and Iraq – with less urbanization, still have great cities with large populations.

Among the issues that define divisions in societies and, in some extreme circumstances, become part of the roots of armed conflict, one that seems to receive surprisingly little attention is the urban/rural divide. Even where populations are homogenous in terms of religion and ethnicity, they may be radically different in their ways of life, depending on whether they live in the cities or outside them. This difference is sometimes a dividing line in conflict, since policies that favour the cities may disadvantage the rural population. But the urban/rural divide is also something that people have to cross in their own ways of life as they go through the process of urbanization – of becoming part of the city.

Urbanization is classically the result of growing economic wealth and industrialization, as people are either forced off the land or leave it in

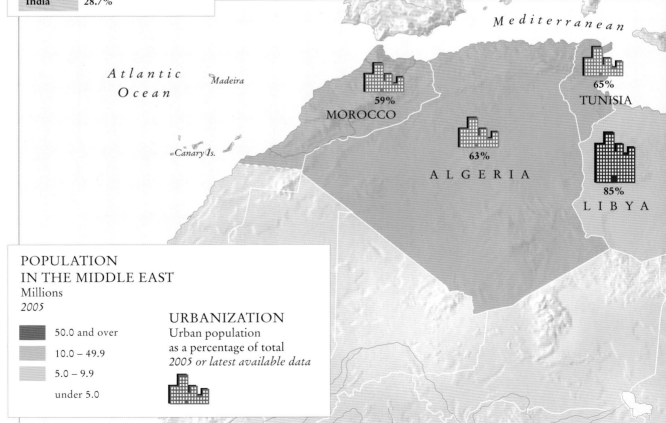

POPULATION IN THE MIDDLE EAST
Millions
2005

	50.0 and over
	10.0 – 49.9
	5.0 – 9.9
	under 5.0

URBANIZATION
Urban population
as a percentage of total
2005 or latest available data

search of new jobs and opportunities in the towns and cities. Urban populations cannot rely on their own farming for their food; they must rely on jobs and wages.

When urbanization happens without commensurate increases in national wealth, there are not enough jobs to provide city-dwellers with adequate family incomes. Urban centres become the places where the flaws of development may be felt most sharply, where what were hopes of betterment end in the bitterest disappointment. It is in the contrast between hope and reality, the relationship between implied opportunity and denied opportunity, that urban unrest grows.

The response to these pressures can take many different forms and be expressed in different ways. One form is that young men migrate to better labour markets in richer countries, there to experience even greater cultural upheaval and to encounter prejudice, discrimination and other new kinds of disadvantage. A different kind of response is to join a political cause at home.

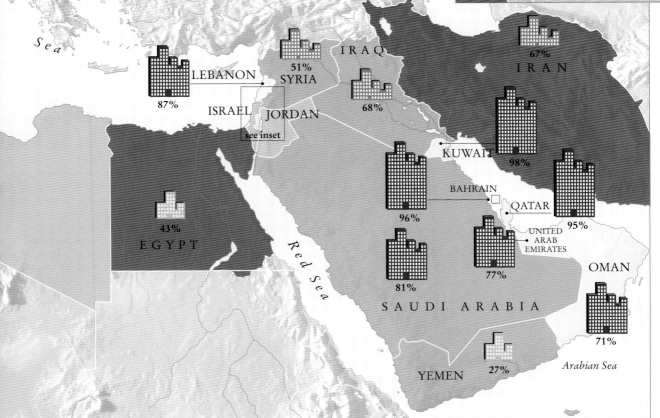

121

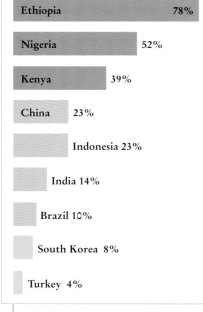

WATER AND SANITATION

Access to clean water and an efficient system of sanitation is one of the basic requirements for healthy living conditions. It is, accordingly, a basic aim for economic and social development, and a revealing indicator of the progress of, and prospects for, development.

While natural sources of water can often be clean and safe, most people, and especially those living in cities, are dependent on social programmes to establish and treat water supplies, pipe it into communities and homes, and then to do the work necessary to maintain these systems. Access to clean water, therefore, is a product both of the availability of natural supplies of water, and of the deployment of economic resources and technology to ensure that the water is clean and distributed amongst the population. The requirement for sanitation in urban environments must likewise be fulfilled collectively. In most cases these needs can only be met by large-scale, state-funded programmes.

By the standards of developing countries, the provision of clean water and sanitation across the Middle East as a whole is not bad. But in some

POOR WATER PROVISION IN THE MIDDLE EAST
Percentage of population without access to an improved water supply
2004 or latest available data

- 20% and over
- 10% – 19%
- under 10%
- no data

SANITATION
More than 15% of population lack adequate sanitation
2004 or latest available data

parts of the region it is seriously inadequate. The overall supply of water is very limited. The Middle East is a dry region and most countries have an average supply of less than 1,000 litres per person per year, which puts them in the lowest bracket worldwide *(see pages 132-33)*. From this difficult starting point, some states in the region have managed to make sure that most of their population has access to clean water; others have not deployed the economic and technological resources to do so.

Water availability in the Middle East is not expected to improve in the coming half century, and several Middle Eastern countries are expected to face chronic shortages by 2050. These countries have a major incentive – both for the welfare of their citizens and for the country's economic development – to take decisive action to ensure that they run efficient and clean public water supply systems. Whether they are successful will do much to define their development prospects in the second half of the 21st century.

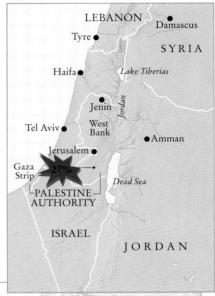

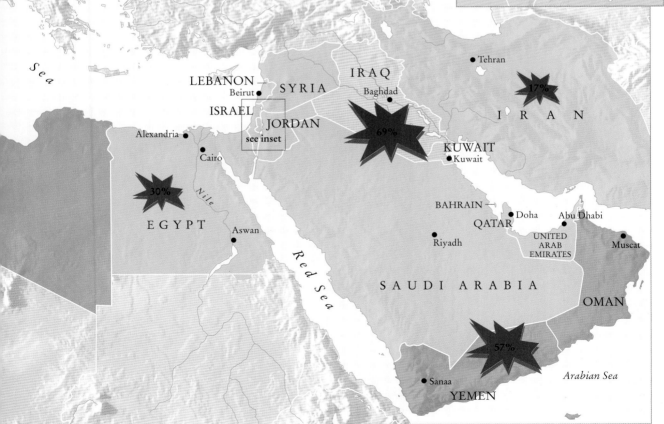

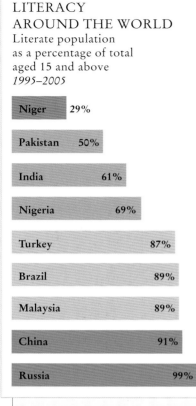

LITERACY AROUND THE WORLD

Literate population
as a percentage of total
aged 15 and above
1995–2005

Country	Literacy
Niger	29%
Pakistan	50%
India	61%
Nigeria	69%
Turkey	87%
Brazil	89%
Malaysia	89%
China	91%
Russia	99%

EDUCATION AND LITERACY

E ducation is both a product and a driving force of development. The richest countries in the world uniformly have functional literacy levels of above 90 percent among people over the age of 15. It is, therefore, indicative of development dilemmas in the Middle East that only Israel shows literacy rates above 90 percent, while the regional norm is between 50 and 90 percent.

In the near future, literacy rates are likely to increase, with just over 80 percent of the region's primary school age children enrolled for education. However, the Middle East's performance is, as in several other development indicators, no better than mid-range: it exceeds the levels of primary-school enrolment in Sub-Saharan Africa and South Asia, while lagging considerably behind Latin America's. There are some signs that a major effort to improve school education in the first part of the 1980s has faded in the last decade and a half. Education expenditure per head of the population has remained roughly stable for two decades while for the world's richest countries it has increased steadily.

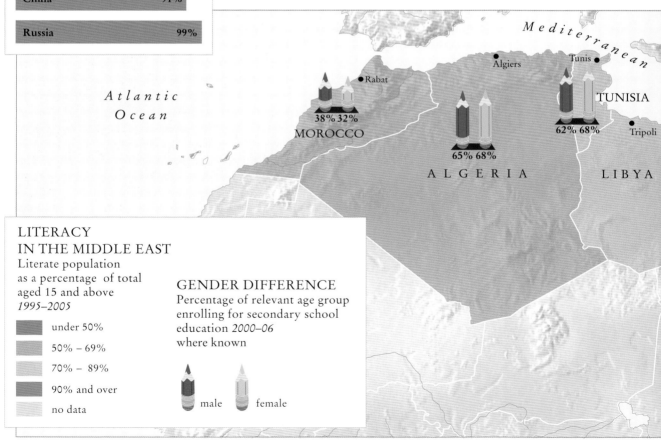

LITERACY IN THE MIDDLE EAST

Literate population
as a percentage of total
aged 15 and above
1995–2005

- under 50%
- 50% – 69%
- 70% – 89%
- 90% and over
- no data

GENDER DIFFERENCE

Percentage of relevant age group
enrolling for secondary school
education *2000–06*
where known

male female

124

The basic functional literacy that is achieved through primary and secondary education is (or should be) the basis for a strong higher education sector. Especially in the Arab countries, the university sector is often criticized for lack of attention to the quality of education provided. Some analysts have traced this to the very high levels of employment in public administration – about ten percent in the Middle East as a whole, more than twice the level in Asia and almost twice that in Latin America. For a region with a university tradition going back several centuries, the research sector is weak by world standards.

Inequality between the two genders has been identified by many commentators as a major deficiency and hindrance to prospects of equitable development. It is therefore worth noting that in several countries the proportions of boys and girls completing primary education are approximately equal, and in some countries there is a higher percentage of girls. In itself this does not signify a coming empowerment of women, but without equal education access for girls there would be very little prospect of greater gender equality.

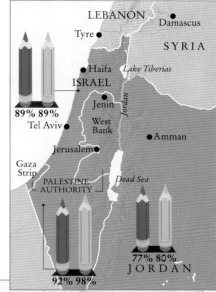

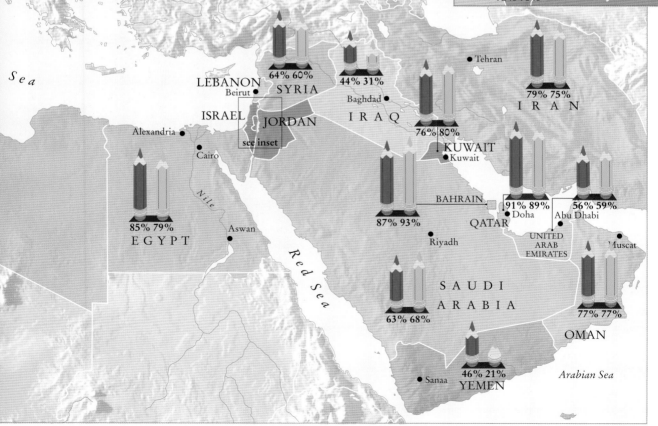

Sierra Leone $806

Nigeria $1,128

India $3,452

Turkey $8,407

Brazil $8,402

South Africa $11,110

South Korea $22,029

France $30,386

USA $41,890

GOVERNMENT
AND ECONOMY

Economic performance and conditions in the Middle East are highly varied. One country – Yemen – falls into the world's poorest category, with annual national income below $1,000 per head. At the other end of the scale, some Gulf states' average income is comparable to European countries', as is Israel's despite its permanent state of military preparedness and the economic consequences of the *intifada*.

For much of the region the dominant economic fact is oil, and large oil reserves have generated enormous wealth. But when world oil prices fell, this dependence on oil income became a liability. Economic performance in the oil-rich countries fluctuates according to variations in world prices and, from one year to the next, prosperity for many ordinary people comes and goes. These peaks and troughs tend to come much closer together than the highs and lows of economic cycles in industrialized countries and induce a condition of permanent instability.

It is a common argument that the Middle East will find stability and development that will benefit the majority of the people only with the establishment of fully fledged democracy. Certainly, despite its flaws,

POLITICAL SYSTEMS
IN THE MIDDLE EAST
2007

- established democracy
- transitional/uncertain democracy
- one-party rule
- monarchy
- theocracy
- dependent territory

GDP PER PERSON
Purchasing Power Parity
in US dollars
2005 or latest available data
where known

democracy offers the possibility of economic and social development that is bothy efficient and relatively fair. But democracy is only real if it grows from within countries, at the urging of the majority of the population. To attempt to democratize countries 'from the outside' is dangerous and has uncertain prospects.

There are elected assemblies in several Middle East countries; they are an outlet for expression of public sentiment on some issues, and in some cases their advisory role is taken seriously but they do not hold executive power. Even in Iran, where the President and Assembly are directly elected, greater power lies in the hands of the religious leadership.

For democracy to be real, the citizens' votes in free and fair elections must decide who holds executive power. Only in Israel has this been the case consistently since independence. In the early years of the 21st century, Lebanon was attempting to rediscover democracy and Yemen had a presidential election in 1999, though the opposition, who took just four percent of the vote, declared it was rigged.

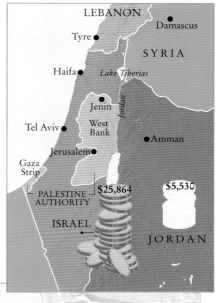

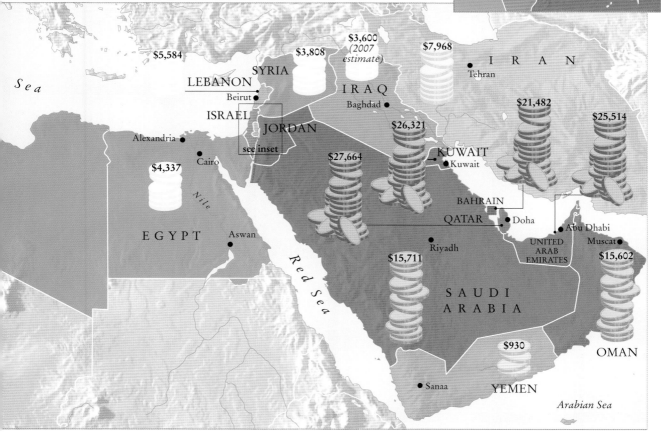

127

MILITARY SPENDING

MILITARY EXPENDITURE
AROUND THE WORLD
Percentage of GDP
2005

Mexico 0.4%

Brazil 1.6%

India 2.8%

Turkey 2.8%

China 2.0%

UK 2.7%

USA 4.1%

Burundi 6.2%

Eritrea   24.1%

In themselves, the percentages of national wealth devoted to military spending in the Middle East may not seem impressive. In fact, those countries that are spending more than five percent of annual income on the military are spending around the same proportion of their wealth on the military as the USA and USSR were during the worst years of the Cold War.

Despite the fact that it provides employment, military spending is an economic burden. Its greatest economic cost lies in lost opportunities for investment and economic growth. The cost would, of course, be justified if there were no other way to find security and as long as it did not rise so high as to actually break the economy.

For most of the countries spending above the five percent mark, that relatively heavy expenditure is simply one more in a range of reasons that explain why economic performance has been disappointing over the past two decades. Whether enough gains in security have been achieved to justify the economic costs is a matter for conjecture and

MILITARY EXPENDITURE
IN THE MIDDLE EAST
Percentage of GDP
2005

- 12% and over
- 9% – 11%
- 5% – 8%
- under 5%
- no data

Parties to the 1968
Nuclear Non-Proliferation Treaty
2007

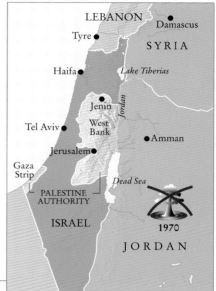

argument. The region has lived in a state of insecurity for decades; relatively high military spending is hardly a surprising response to that ambient sense of danger – but nor does it yet seem to have been a successful response. Radically reducing military spending is a risk that most states are highly unlikely to take until security problems have been resolved; relying on military means alone to provide security would be an equal risk.

When Iraq's international isolation in the 1990s meant it dropped out of many kinds of global data collection and comparison, one of the big question marks concerned the size of its armed forces and military spending. During the war with Iran in 1980–88, Iraq spent an unsustainable 40 percent of national wealth on the military. By 2000, it was estimated to be spending about ten percent. However, its economy had shrivelled under the impact of wars and sanctions, and its annual military spending was less than half that of Kuwait or the UAE.

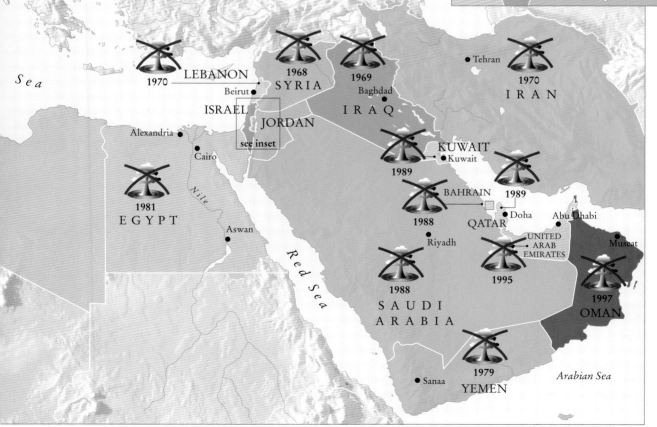

ENERGY USE AROUND THE WORLD

Oil consumption
barrels per 1,000 people per day
2007

USA 68.8

UK 30.1

Russia 17.7

Brazil 11.1

China 4.9

India 2.2

Kenya 1.5

ENERGY AND TRANSPORTATION

Economic history reveals a parabolic or bell-shaped pattern in many key indicators of development. Population, for example, tends to increase sharply with economic development, because as conditions improve infant mortality declines and people live longer. After a while, however, increasing prosperity encourages people to have fewer children, so population growth slows and stops.

Likewise with energy: its use increases with economic development, because every activity that adds economic value consumes energy, and as prosperity is spread more widely so, for example, more people have cars, as well as central heating in cooler climates and air-conditioning, which is particularly energy intensive, in the heat. After a while, however, continuing development and technological sophistication means that the consumption of energy can be moderated, and some of the most energy-intensive activities in heavy industry get relocated from rich countries to poorer countries where development is just taking off.

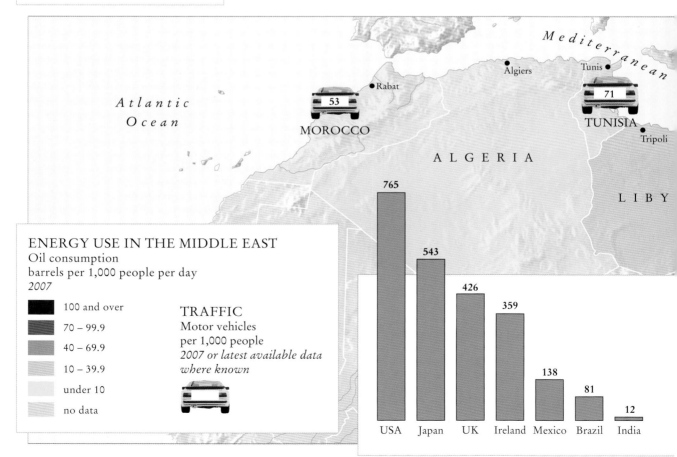

Atlantic Ocean

Mediterranean

Algiers • Tunis •

• Rabat

53

MOROCCO

71

TUNISIA

Tripoli

A L G E R I A

L I B Y

ENERGY USE IN THE MIDDLE EAST

Oil consumption
barrels per 1,000 people per day
2007

- 100 and over
- 70 – 99.9
- 40 – 69.9
- 10 – 39.9
- under 10
- no data

TRAFFIC

Motor vehicles
per 1,000 people
*2007 or latest available data
where known*

USA	Japan	UK	Ireland	Mexico	Brazil	India
765	543	426	359	138	81	12

130

Most Middle Eastern countries are currently on the upward slope with rising energy consumption. In most countries for which statistics are available, personal use of cars is at levels comparable with Latin America and, at the higher end, western Europe.

The very high consumption of energy in Qatar and UAE reflects not only those countries' overall economic development but also their intensive construction programmes to provide luxury resorts for top dollar tourism. Because attracting international tourists in the Middle East requires, among other things, air-conditioned hotels, apartment complexes, entertainment centres and shopping malls, their energy consumption is likely to remain high.

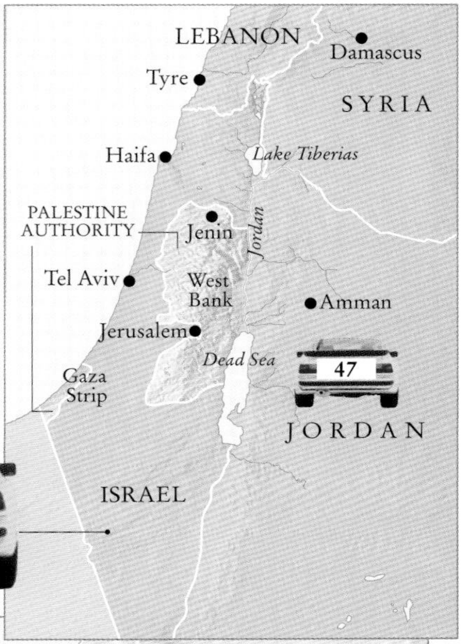

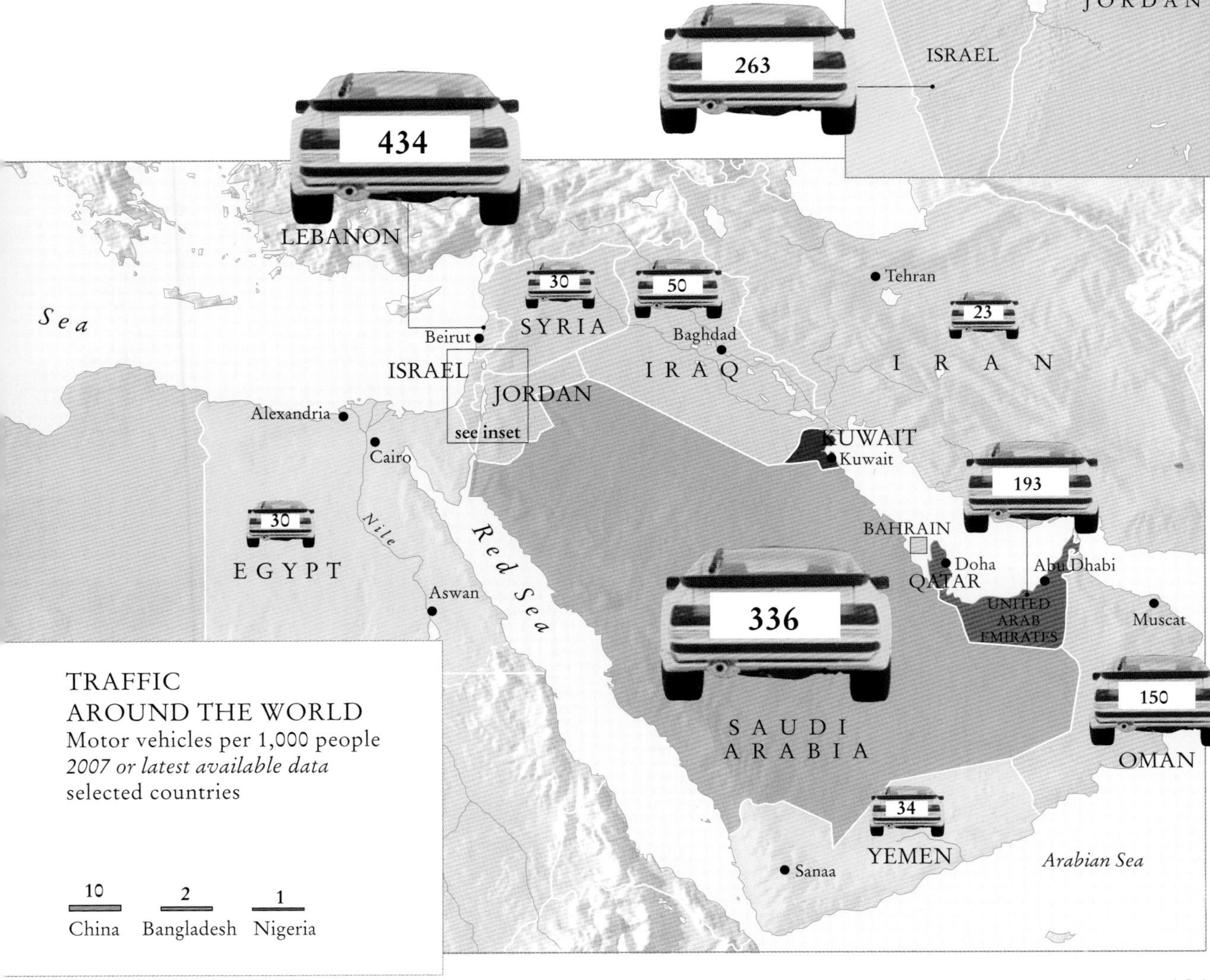

LEBANON
Damascus
Tyre
SYRIA
Haifa
Lake Tiberias
PALESTINE
AUTHORITY — Jenin
Jordan
Tel Aviv
West
Bank
Amman
Jerusalem
Dead Sea
47
Gaza
Strip
JORDAN
ISRAEL

263

434

LEBANON

Sea

Beirut
30
SYRIA
50
Tehran
23
ISRAEL
Baghdad
I R A Q
I R A N
JORDAN
see inset
KUWAIT
Kuwait
Alexandria
Cairo
BAHRAIN
193
Nile
Doha
Abu Dhabi
QATAR
Red Sea
UNITED
ARAB
EMIRATES
Muscat
EGYPT
336
Aswan

TRAFFIC
AROUND THE WORLD
Motor vehicles per 1,000 people
2007 or latest available data
selected countries

SAUDI
ARABIA

150

OMAN

34
YEMEN
Arabian Sea

Sanaa

10	2	1
China	Bangladesh	Nigeria

RENEWABLE WATER RESOURCES AROUND THE WORLD
Cubic metres available
per person per year
2007 or latest available data

Bahamas	66
Maldives	103
Kenya	985
Denmark	1,128
South Africa	1,154
India	1,880
France	3,439
Turkey	3,439
USA	7,407

WATER RESOURCES

Water is essential for human life. Worldwide, the supply of water for human consumption has reached a critical point. Almost 60 countries may face chronic water shortages by 2050; among them are most of the countries in the Middle East – the exceptions being Iran, Iraq, Lebanon and Morocco.

The importance of water as a source of life, wealth and power means that it is therefore a source of conflict. In Israel, the West Bank and Gaza the imbalance in the use of water is a constant source of resentment for Palestinians. Among the issues in the background of the 1967 Arab-Israeli war was the concern in the Israeli government about a proposal by Jordan to divert the flow of the River Jordan. Israel was founded in part on the basis of irrigating and farming the desert; water is a particularly sensitive issue of national security. By taking control of the West Bank in 1967, Israel not only gained access to the river but also to the area's underground water sources.

Water is a potential conflict issue in other areas too. Egypt is supplied

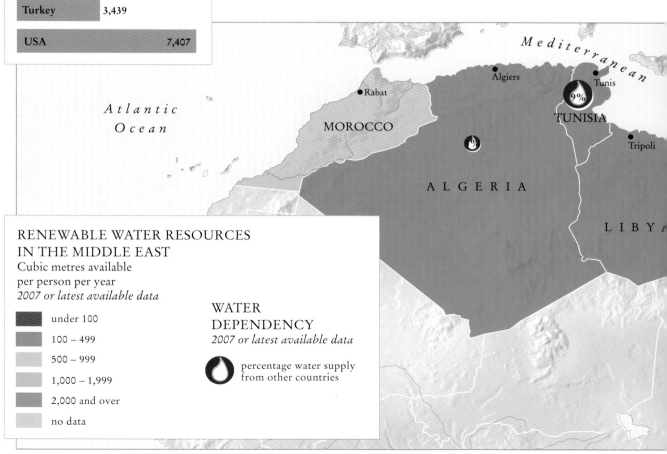

RENEWABLE WATER RESOURCES IN THE MIDDLE EAST
Cubic metres available
per person per year
2007 or latest available data

- under 100
- 100 – 499
- 500 – 999
- 1,000 – 1,999
- 2,000 and over
- no data

WATER DEPENDENCY
2007 or latest available data

⬤ percentage water supply from other countries

by the Nile – a source of wealth but also of vulnerability. Downstream states are always vulnerable to upstream states deciding to dam or divert major rivers. Iraq and Syria are both dependent on the Tigris and the Euphrates, both of which rise in Turkey.

Control of water is also used as a weapon in war. Palestinian groups attempted to disrupt Israel's water supplies during the second *intifada* and Israel retaliated in kind. During the 1980–88 war against Iraq, Iran diverted rivers to flood Iraqi positions and bombed dams in Kurdistan. Iraq itself destroyed Kuwait's desalination plants in 1991 after its invasion, and Saddam Hussein first poisoned the water source for the Marsh Arabs in southern Iraq during the 1990s, and then systematically drained the areas where they lived.

However, water can also be a source of peace and cooperation. There is a growing network of international agreements around the River Nile, and no reason – in principle – why the same could not happen around the Tigris and the Euphrates.

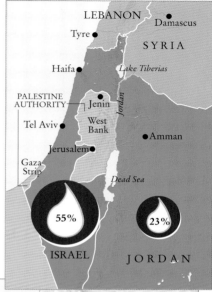

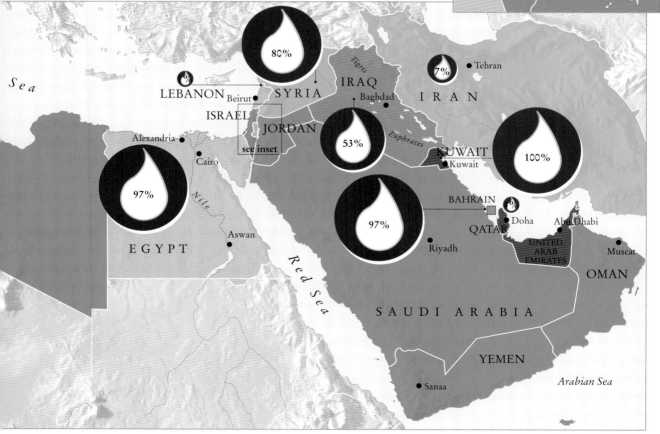

CROSS-BORDER MIGRATION AROUND THE WORLD

People born outside the country excluding refugees
as a percentage of total population
2000

Australia	24.3%
Switzerland	24.3%
USA	12.2%
UK	6.6%
India	0.6%
Mexico	0.5%
Brazil	0.3%
China	0.1%

LABOUR AND MIGRATION

There is a push-and-pull basis to labour migration. Lack of opportunities means workers look outside their national borders for work – the push effect – and they choose where to go on the basis of information about the best employment prospects – the pull. In the Middle East, the small oil-rich states of the Gulf exercise the greatest pulling power, drawing within the region on countries like Egypt and Yemen as well as on countries such as Pakistan outside the region. France and other European countries are the main destinations for labour migration from Morocco, Algeria and Tunisia.

One consequence of labour migration within the region is that the economic effects of fluctuating oil prices reach beyond the oil-rich countries. Economic well-being in countries that lack natural reserves of oil is linked to oil prices by the remittances sent home by migrant workers in the oil states. When prices go up and the oil-rich get richer, they need more workers; when prices go down, foreign workers lose their jobs and get sent home.

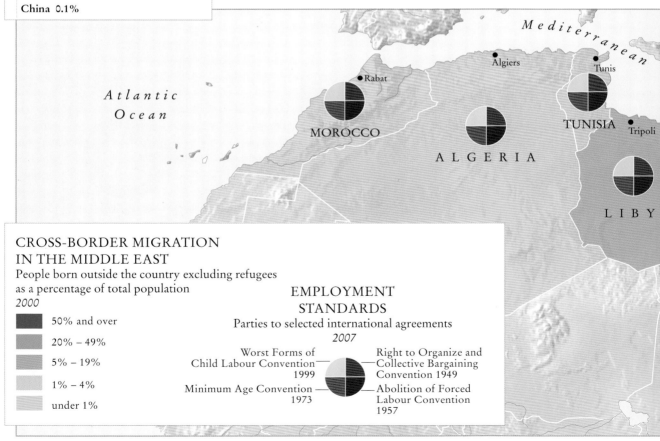

CROSS-BORDER MIGRATION IN THE MIDDLE EAST

People born outside the country excluding refugees
as a percentage of total population
2000

- 50% and over
- 20% – 49%
- 5% – 19%
- 1% – 4%
- under 1%

EMPLOYMENT STANDARDS

Parties to selected international agreements
2007

Worst Forms of Child Labour Convention 1999

Right to Organize and Collective Bargaining Convention 1949

Minimum Age Convention 1973

Abolition of Forced Labour Convention 1957

Despite the vagaries of the system, Egypt and Yemen have been able to get by on the basis of money earned abroad and sent home. Over the longer term, as populations grow, if there is a persistent lack of economic opportunities at home, the consequences will be felt in social problems and the resentment of the next generation.

For workers who move from one Arab country to another, the fact that the same language is spoken might help ease the difficulties of transition and acceptance that migrants always face. Problems persist nonetheless because though the written language is shared, dialect and accent mark the newcomer out as different. Where immigrants form a large section of the population, the capacity for an eventual explosion of rage is as great in the Middle East as in European countries.

Workers' rights in those countries in the region that attract the most labour migration are in general deficient by international standards, and implementation often falls far short of the paper commitments the government has made.

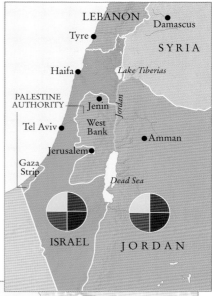

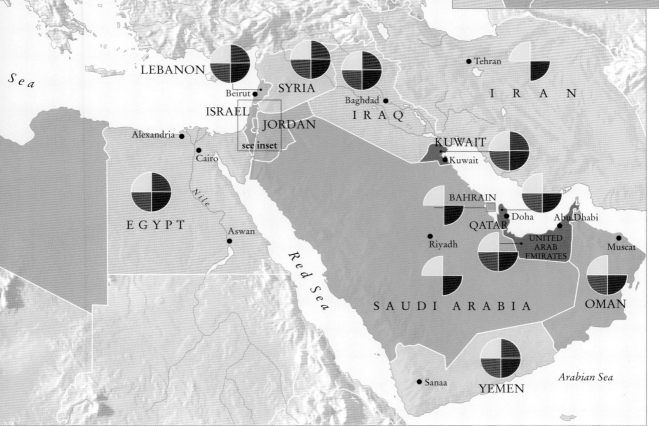

REFUGEES

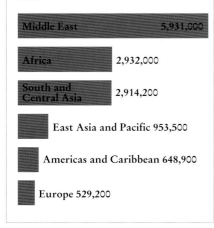
Palestinians form the largest single group of refugees in the world, constituting by themselves more than a quarter of the world's total of cross-border refugees, and about one tenth of the total number of people who have been made homeless by war. Among Palestinians living in the Middle East, refugees account for almost half of the total.

Jordan remains host to the largest number of Palestinian refugees and large numbers also went to, and have remained in, Lebanon and Syria. Iran has hosted very large numbers of Afghan refugees during the years of foreign intervention and civil war since 1979.

There were two great waves of refugee flight by Palestinians. The first came with the foundation of Israel in 1948, when 80 percent of Palestinians within the new borders left. Statistics on refugees are notoriously unreliable and often hotly contested. The international comparisons on this map use data from a different source than the figures for Palestinian refugees on page 56. They come from the UN Relief and Works Agency, which offers figures only on Palestinian refugees. Because the different sources use different definitions, the figure for Palestinian refugees in Jordan on this map is markedly lower than that on page 56. The second wave of refugee flight by Palestinians came with Israel's occupation of the West Bank as a result of the Six Day War in 1967. Living outside their homeland as refugees has become a semi-permanent condition for millions of Palestinians and has lasted for two generations since the original flight in 1948. The term 'refugee *camp*' has become a misnomer with its implication of impermanence.

When peace agreements are reached, it is normal for refugees to return home – not only are they allowed to do so, but it is regarded as a right and they are encouraged and assisted to return. While the issue of refugee return remains a paramount question for Palestinians, many Israelis see it as a source of danger. Outsiders can regard the intractability of this question as a symptom of the difficulties of arriving at a mutually acceptable peace settlement.

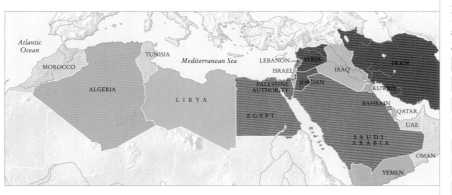

REFUGEES
IN THE MIDDLE EAST
Number of cross-border refugees
and asylum seekers
2006

- over 1,000,000
- 500,000 – 1,000,000
- 100,000 – 499,999
- 50,000 – 99,999
- 10,000 – 49,999
- under 5,000
- no data

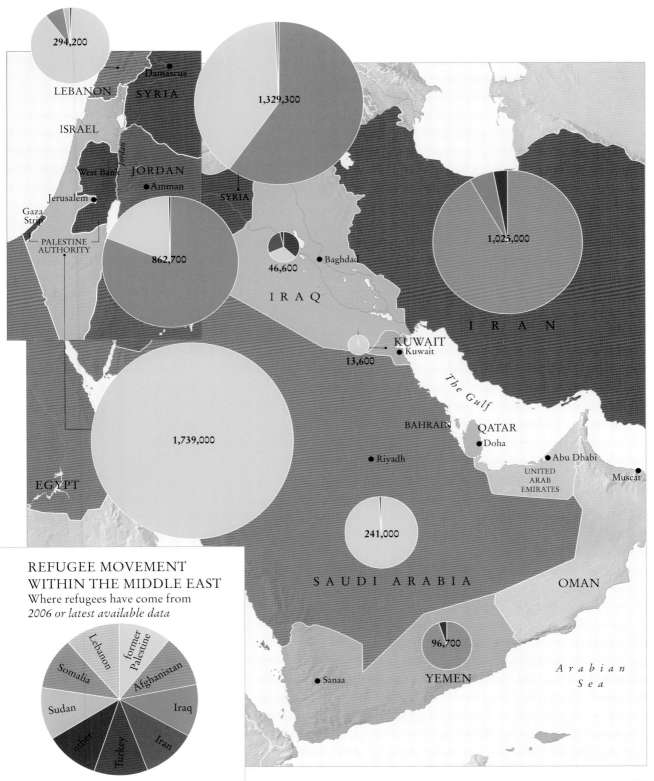

294,200

LEBANON   SYRIA
•Damascus

ISRAEL

West Bank   JORDAN
Jerusalem •   •Amman

Gaza
Strip
PALESTINE
AUTHORITY

1,329,300

SYRIA

862,700

46,600   •Baghdad

I R A Q

1,025,000

I R A N

KUWAIT
13,600   •Kuwait

The Gulf

1,739,000

BAHRAIN   QATAR
•Doha

•Riyadh

UNITED
ARAB   •Abu Dhabi
EMIRATES   •Muscat

EGYPT

241,000

SAUDI ARABIA   OMAN

REFUGEE MOVEMENT
WITHIN THE MIDDLE EAST
Where refugees have come from
2006 or latest available data

96,700

YEMEN

*Arabian
Sea*

•Sanaa

former
Palestine
Lebanon
Afghanistan
Somalia
Iraq
Sudan
Iran
other
Turkey

137

GENDER EQUALITY

Throughout the world, women face significant disadvantages compared to men, with lower paid work, less access to positions of power and influence, less active participation in politics. In many countries the gap is narrowing and discrimination against women is not so widely enshrined in law.

The *Arab Human Development Report* has identified three key deficits in Arab societies – deficits of freedom, knowledge and empowerment of women. The recognition that the lack of gender equality is one of the key issues defining the region's development prospects could mark a major step forward in thinking about the dilemmas of development in the Arab world.

The degree of inequality between men and women varies significantly within the region, and in some cases the situation looks quite self-contradictory. Most countries have universal suffrage, but in Lebanon women may vote only if they have had elementary education, and in Kuwait and Saudi Arabia only men may vote. Yet Kuwait, despite

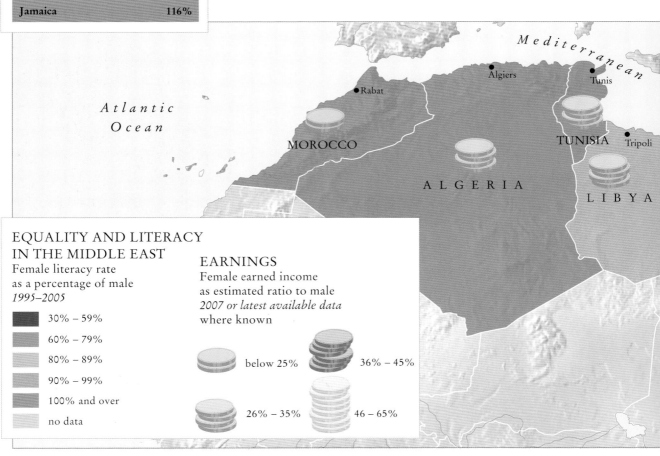

EQUALITY AND LITERACY IN THE MIDDLE EAST

Female literacy rate
as a percentage of male
1995–2005

- 30% – 59%
- 60% – 79%
- 80% – 89%
- 90% – 99%
- 100% and over
- no data

EARNINGS

Female earned income
as estimated ratio to male
2007 or latest available data
where known

- below 25%
- 26% – 35%
- 36% – 45%
- 46 – 65%

that institutionalized discrimination against women, is one of the Arab countries where there have been great advances in recent decades and the literacy rates for men and women are similar.

The unfair conditions faced by women are defined not only by law and state policy, but also by social norms and customs. In many countries women who have been raped face the risk of murder by their own relatives to expunge the 'shame' caused by a male act of aggression. Both the local community and the authorities often turn a blind eye to these merciless killings.

In several Arab countries and also in Iran, the participation of women in public life is constrained by systems of governance that tightly control who may lead. Only Israel has so far produced a female political leader – Golda Meir from 1969 to 1974. In terms of women's rights and conditions, Israel is much closer to countries of Europe and North America and in some respects – the employment of female soldiers, for example – can claim to have led the way.

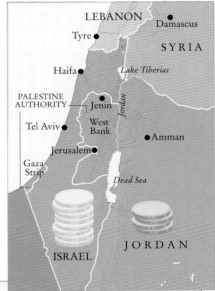

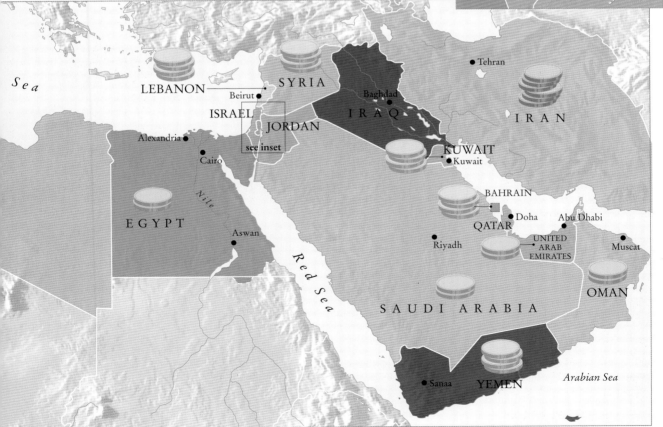

HUMAN RIGHTS

Human rights abuse is widespread in the Middle East, a product of the region's combination of wars, arbitrary systems of power and government, inequality and social exclusion.

What is worse is that this is a vicious cycle. Gross abuses of human rights, of the kinds recorded on this map, also contribute to the conditions of war, arbitrary power, inequality and exclusion. The combination of inadequate human security and a lack of good governance – a dual deficiency that is epitomized in the gross abuse of human rights – is a major blockage impeding efficient and sustainable economic development.

In some senses, then, this map encapsulates the consequences of the underlying problems of the region. Were it possible in the future to draw a comparable map for the region and find a significant decline in human rights abuse, that would be *prima facie* evidence that several states had begun to resolve the key development problems. To some degree, the map understates the problem. The way the map works is that it shows

HUMAN RIGHTS IN THE MIDDLE EAST
2006
States whose reported abuses of human rights include:

- extra-judicial executions
- torture
- arbitrary arrest and detention
- mistreatment by police and/or prison authorities

PROTECTION
Parties to selected international agreements
2007

Convention on the Rights of the Child 1989

International Convention on the Prevention and Punishment of the Crime of Genocide 1948

Convention against Torture and Other Cruel, Inhuman or Degrading Treatment or Punishment 1984

Convention on the Elimination of All Forms of Discrimination against Women 1979

the worst abuses in each state. In general, where extra-judicial executions occur, so does torture, and where there is torture there is usually a pattern of arbitrary arrest and detention, and so on.

It is against this background that the actions of the occupying forces of the USA and Britain in Iraq can be more fully assessed. The well-documented cases of human rights abuse by those forces, which have been investigated by US and British authorities, are not wrong only because they seriously abuse the rights and dignity of the men who were trampled on, led around naked on leashes and threatened with further humiliation and degradation. Nor is the problem that they diminish the credibility and tarnish the image of the whole intervention in Iraq.

The real crime is that they add to the pervasive reality – of which ordinary Iraqis have all too much experience – that those in power abuse human rights and disregard international law. With this, the occupying forces have simply contributed to the long list of obstacles that make social and economic development so difficult for Iraq.

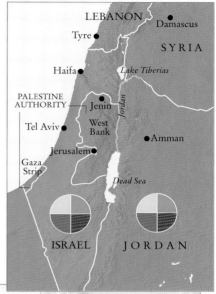

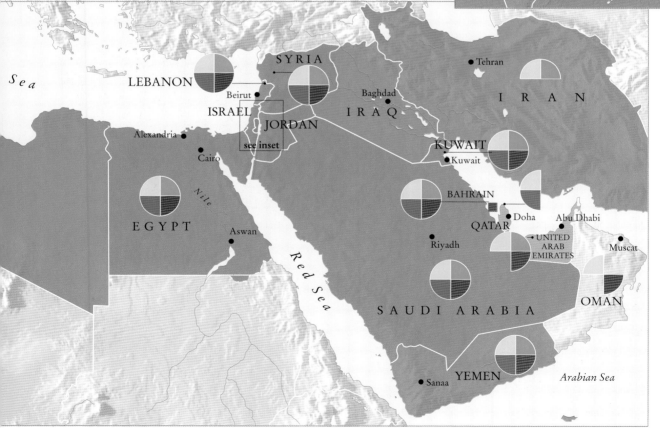

SOURCES

NEWS SOURCES
Al-Jazeera, BBC, PBS, Reuters, The Economist, The Financial Times, The Guardian, The New York Times, The Times.

REPORTS, YEARBOOKS AND OFFICIAL PUBLICATIONS
Amnesty International, *Amnesty International Report*, 2003, 2004, 2005, London.

Europa Publications, *Europa World Yearbook*, 2005, Routledge/Taylor & Francis, London.

HMG, *Palestine: Statement of Policy by His Majesty's Government in the United Kingdom* 1937, His Majesty's Stationary Office, London.

HMG, *Palestine: Statement of Policy by His Majesty's Government in the United Kingdom,* 1938, His Majesty's Stationary Office, London.

HMG, *Palestine: Statement of Policy by His Majesty's Government in the United Kingdom,* 1939, His Majesty's Stationary Office, London.

Human Security Centre, *Human Security Report*, 2005, Oxford University Press, New York.

International Crisis Group, Can Saudi Arabia reform itself?, *Middle East and North Africa Report 28*, 14 July 2004, Cairo/Brussels.

International Crisis Group, Islamism in North Africa I: the legacies of history, *Middle East and North Africa Briefing*, 20 April 2004, Cairo/Brussels.

International Crisis Group, Islamism in North Africa II: Egypt's opportunity, *Middle East and North Africa Briefing*, 20 April 2004, Cairo/Brussels.

International Crisis Group, Islamism, violence and reform in Algeria: turning the page, *Middle East and North Africa Report 29*, 30 July 2004, Cairo/Brussels.

International Crisis Group, Reforming Egypt: in search of a strategy, *Middle East and North Africa Report 46*, October 2005, Cairo/Brussels.

International Crisis Group, Saudi Arabia backgrounder: who are the Islamists?, *Middle East and North Africa Report 31*, 21 September 2004, Cairo/Brussels.

International Crisis Group, *Israel/Hizbollah/Lebanon: Avoiding Renewed Conflict*, Middle East Report N°59, 1 November 2006.

International Crisis Group, *After Baker-Hamilton: What to Do in Iraq*, Middle East Report N°60, 19 December 2006.

International Crisis Group, *Iraq and the Kurds: Resolving the Kirkuk Crisis*, Middle East Report N°64, 19 April 2007.

International Crisis Group, *After Gaza,* Middle East Report N°68, 2 August 2007.

International Crisis Group, *Where Is Iraq Heading? Lessons from Basra*, Middle East Report N°67, 25 June 2007.

International Crisis Group, *Hizbollah and the Lebanese Crisis*, Middle East Report N°69, 10 October 2007, Brussels.

International Crisis Group, *Shiite Politics in Iraq: The Role of the Supreme Council*, Middle East Report N°70, 15 November 2007.

International Crisis Group, *Iraq's Civil War, the Sadrists and the Surge*, Middle East Report N°72, 7 February 2008.

International Institute for Strategic Studies, *Strategic Survey*, 2005, Routledge/Taylor & Francis, London.

International Institute for Strategic Studies, *The Military Balance 2001-2002*, 2001, IISS Publications, London.

International Institute for Strategic Studies, *The Military Balance 2004-2005*, 2004, IISS Publications, London.

International Institute for Strategic Studies, *The Military Balance 2008*, 2008 IISS Publications.

International Institute for Strategic Studies, *The Baghdad Surge*, IISS Publications/IISS Strategic Comments, May 2007.

D McDowall, *Minority Rights Group Report: The Kurds*, 1997, Minority Rights Group, London.

Palestine Partition Commission, *Report*, 1938, His Majesty's Stationary Office, London.

SIPRI, *Yearbook 2005: Armaments, Disarmament and International Security*, 2005 Oxford University Press, Oxford.

UN Development Programme, *Arab Human Development Report*, 2002, New York.

UN Development Programme, *Human Development Reports*, 2003 and 2005, Oxford University Press, Oxford, New York.

UN Development Programme, *Egypt Human Development Report*, 2004, Commercial Press, Kalyoub.

UN Office for the Coordination of Humanitarian Affairs, *West Bank Closure Count and Analysis*, 2006, East Jerusalem.

BOOKS
S Abu Sitta, *Atlas of Palestine 1948*, 2005, Palestine Land Society, London.

M J Akbar, *The Shade of Swords*, 2002, Routledge, London.

K Armstrong, *Muhammad: A Biography of the Prophet*, 1991, Phoenix Press, London.

K Armstrong, *A History of Jerusalem*, 1997, HarperCollins, London.

K Armstrong, *Islam: A Short History*, 2000, Phoenix Press, London.

K Armstrong, *Holy War*, 2001, Anchor Books, New York.

N N Ayubi, *Over-Stating the Arab State: Politics and Society in the Middle East*, 1995, IB Tauris, London.

H Blix, *Disarming Iraq*, 2004, Bloomsbury, London.

M van Bruinesen, *Aga, Shaikh & State*, 1992, Zed Press, London.

R A Clarke, *Against All Enemies*, 2004, Free Press, New York.

W L Cleveland, *A History of the Modern Middle East*, 1994, Westview Press, Boulder, Colorado.

A Cockburn & P Cockburn, *Saddam Hussein: And American Obsession*, 2002, Verso, London.

A H Cordesman, *Energy Developments in the Middle East*, 2004, Praeger Publishers, Westport, CT.

A H Cordesman, *Saudi Arabia : Guarding the Desert Kingdom*, 1997, Westview Press, Boulder, Colorado.

A Dawisha, *Arab Nationalism in the Twentieth Century: From Triumph to Despair*, 2005, Princeton University Press, Princeton, New Jersey.

J L Esposito, *Unholy War: Terror in the Name of Islam*, 2005, Oxford University Press, New York.

R Fisk, *Pity the Nation: Lebanon at War*, 2001, Oxford University Press, Oxford, 3rd edn.

R Fisk, *The Great War for Civilisation*, 2005, Fourth Estate, London.

A Friedman & N Rami eds, *Divided Cities in Transition*, 2003, International Peace & Cooperation Centre / Jerusalem Institute for Israel Studies, Jerusalem.

D Fromkin, *A Peace to End all Peace*, 2000, Phoenix Press, London.

P W Galbraith, *The End of Iraq*, Simon Schuster, New York, 2006

M Gilbert, *The Routledge Atlas of the Arab-Israeli Conflict*, 2002, Routledge, London, 7th edn.

M Gilbert, *Israel: A History*, 1999, Black Swan, London.

M Gilsenan, *Recognising Islam. Religion and Society in the Modern Middle East*, 2000, IB Tauris, London.

R Gunaratna, *Inside Al Qaeda*, 2002, Hurst & Co, London.

S M Hersh, *Chain of Command*, 2005, Penguin, London.

A Hertzberg, *The Zionist Idea*, 1930, 1997, The Jewish Publication Society, Philadelphia.

T Herzl, *The Jewish State*, 1988, Dover Publications, New York.

J Holmes, *Fallujah*, Constable, London 2007.

A Hourani, *A History of the Arab Peoples*, 1991, Faber & Faber, London.

A Hourani, *Arabic Thought in the Liberal Age 1798-1939*, 1962, 1983, Cambridge University Press, Cambridge.

M Isikoff & D Corn, *Hubris*, Crown, New York, 2006.

J Keegan, *The Iraq War*, 2004, Hutchinson, London.

G Kepel, *Jihad: The Trail of Political Islam*, 2002, IB Tauris, London.

R Khalidi, *Resurrecting Empire*, 2004, Beacon Press, Boston, MT.

R Khalidi, *The Iron Cage*, Beacon Press, Boston, 2006.

R Kapuscinski, *Shah of Shahs*, Penguin, London, 1985.

S Al-Khalil, *Republic of Fear: The Inside Story of Saddam's Iraq*, 1990, Pantheon, New York.

B Kimmerling, *Politicide: Ariel Sharon's War against the Palestinians*, 2003, Verso, London.

Baron JPD Kinross, *The Ottoman Centuries*, 2002, Perennial, New York.

B Lewis, *The Crisis of Islam*, 2003, Phoenix Press, London.

B Lewis, *What Went Wrong?*, 2002, Weidenfeld & Nicolson, London.

B Lia, *The Society of Muslim Brothers in Egypt: The Rise of an Islamic Mass Movement 1928-1942*, 1998, Garnet Publishing, London.

N Lochery, *Why Blame Israel?*, 2004, Icon Books, Cambridge.

D McDowall, *A Modern History of the Kurds*, 1997, IB Tauris, London.

A Mango, *Ataturk*, 1999, John Murray, London.

A Mango, *The Turks Today*, John Murray, London, 2004.

P Mansfield, *A History of the Middle East*, 2003, Penguin, London, 2nd edn.

S Mishal & A Sela, *The Palestinian Hamas*, Columbia University Press, New York, 2006.

B Morris, *The Birth of the Palestinian Refugee Problem Revisited*, 2004, Cambridge University Press, Cambridge.

R Mottahedeh, *The Mantle of the Prophet*, 2000, One World, Oxford.

National Geographic, *National Geographic Atlas of the Middle East*, 2003, Washington, DC.

V Nasr, *The Shia Revival,* WW Norton, London, 2007 .

M Nisan, *Minorities in the Middle East*, 2002, McFarland, Jefferson, NC, 2nd edn.

A R Norton, *Hizbollah*, Princeton, Princeton University Press, 2007.

J J Norwich, *A Short History of Byzantium*, 1999, Vintage Books, New York.

M B Oren, *Six Days of War. June 1967 and the Making of the Modern Middle East*, 2003, Penguin Books, London.

R Owen, *State, Power and Politics in the Making of the Modern Middle East*, 2000, Routledge, London.

A Palmer, *The Decline and Fall of the Ottoman Empire*, 1992, John Murray, London.

R A Pape, *Dying to Win: The Strategic Logic of Suicide Terrorism*, 2005, Random House, New York.

I Pappe, *A History of Modern Palestine*, 2004, Cambridge University Press, Cambridge.

J Reinharz & A Shapira, *Essential Papers on Zionism*, 1996, Cassell, London.

J Risen, *State of War*, 2006, Free Press, New York.

S Ritter, *Iraq Confidential*, 2005, IB Tauris, London.

E Rogan & A Shlaim eds, *The War for Palestine*, 2001, Cambridge University Press, Cambridge.

M Ruthven, *A Fury for God*, 2002, Granta, London.

N Shepherd, *Ploughing the Sand: British Rule in Palestine*, 1999, John Murray, London.

G Shimoni, *The Zionist Ideology*, 1995, University Press of New England, London.

A Shlaim, *The Iron Wall: Israel and the Arab World*, 2001, Penguin, London.

E Sivan, *Radical Islam. Medieval Theology and Modern Politics*, 1990, Yale University Press, Yale.

Z Sternhell, *The Founding Myths of Israel*, 2001, Princeton University Press, Princeton, New Jersey.

C Unger, *House of Bush, House of Saud*, 2004, Gibson Square Books, London.

E Weinberger, *What I Heard about Iraq*, 2005, Verso, London.

E Weizman, *Hollow Land: Israel's Architecture of Occupation*, Verso, London, 2007

R Wellhausen ed, *Global Risk Outlook 2006*, 2005, Exclusive Analysis, London.

B Woodward, *State of Denial: Bush at War Part III*, Simon Schuster, New York, 2006

B Woodward, *Plan of Attack*, 2004, Simon & Schuster, New York.

M E Yapp, *The Making of the Modern Near East 1792-1923*, 1987, Longman, London.

M E Yapp, *The Near East Since the First World War*, 1996, Longman, New York.

E J Zürcher, *Turkey: A Modern History*, 1998, IB Tauris, London.

JOURNAL ARTICLES

Brig N Alwyn-Foster, Changing the army for counterinsurgency operations, *Military Review*, November/December 2005: 2-15.

A Baram, Saddam Husayn between his power base and the international community, *Middle East Review of International Affairs*, December 2000, 4 (4), also at: http://meria.idc.ac.il/journal/2000/issue4/jv4n4a2.html

I Blumi, The Islamist challenge in Kosova, *Current History*, March 2003, 102 (662): 124-128.

C Boucek, Libyan state-sponsored terrorism: a historical perspective, *Terrorism Monitor*, March 2005, 3 (6).

A Dawisha, Requiem for Arab nationalism, *The Middle East Quarterly*, Winter 2003, 10 (1).

T Dodge, The Causes of US Failure in Iraq, *Survival*, vol.49, no. 1, spring 2007, pp 85-106.

J D Fearon, Iraq's Civil War, *Foreign Affairs*, March/April 2007.

S Hersh, The redirection, *The New Yorker*, 5 March 2007.

H Khashan, Revitalizing Arab nationalism, *The Middle East Quarterly*, March 2000, 7 (1).

P Robins, Can Gulf monarchies survive the oil bust?, *Middle East Quarterly*, December 1994, 1 (4).

M Rodenbeck, A survey of Saudi Arabia, *The Economist*, London, 7 January 2006.

G Stansfield, Accepting Realities in Iraq, *Chatham House Middle East Briefing Paper*, May 2007.

Lt Cdr Y Aboul-Enein, The Egyptian-Yemen war (1962-67): Egyptian perspectives on guerilla warfare, *The U.S. Army Professional Writing Collection*, January/February 2004, also at: http://www.army.mil/professionalwriting/volumes/volume2/march_2004/3_04_3.html

R Youngs, Europe's flawed approach to Arab democracy, *Centre for European Reform Essays*, October 2006.

ELECTRONIC SOURCES

BBC Country Profiles
http://news.bbc.co.uk/2/hi/country_profiles/default.stm
BBC Profile: Algeria's Salafist group
http://news.bbc.co.uk/1/hi/world/africa/3027621.stm
BBC Timelines
http://www.bbc.co.uk/history/timelines/

BP Statistical Review of World Energy 2004
http://www.bp.com/liveassets/bp_internet/globalbp/globalbp_uk_english/publications/energy_reviews/STAGING/local_assets/downloads/pdf/statistical_review_of_world_energy_full_report_2004.pdf
BP Statistical Review of World Energy 2007
http://www.bp.com/productlanding.do?categoryId=6848&contentId=7033471
British Prime Minister's Office
List of Al Qaida inspired terror attacks, July 2005: http://www.number-10.gov.uk/output/Page7930.asp
Brookings Institution Iraq Index
http://www.brookings.edu/iraqindex
CIA World Factbook
http://www.cia.gov/cia/publications/factbook/geos/ag.html
Country Studies Series
Libya and Arab Unity: http://www.country-studies.com/libya/libya-and-arab-unity.html
CRS Issue Brief for Congress
Egypt-United States Relations, 7 March 2005: http://www.fas.org/sgp/crs/mideast/IB93087.pdf
2 April 2003: http://www.fas.org/asmp/resources/govern/crs-ib93087.pdf
Encyclopaedia of the Orient
http://i-cias.com
FAO Water Report 23: Review of world water resources by country: http://www.fao.org/waicent/faoinfo/agricult/agl/aglw/aquastat/water_res/index.stm
Foreign and Commonwealth Office
Country Profiles:
http://www.fco.gov.uk/servlet/Front?pagename=OpenMarket/Xcelerate/ShowPage&c=Page&cid=1007029394365
Global Insight
Economic and financial data: http://www.globalinsight.com/
Global Security
Security information: http://www.globalsecurity.org
International Crisis Group
Middle East & North Africa reports: http://www.crisisgroup.org/home/index.cfm?id=1096&l=1
International Labour Organization
http://www.ilo.org
IslamiCity
http://www.islamicity.com
Islam and Islamic history in Arabia and the Middle East: the coming of the West: http://www.islamicity.com/mosque/ihame/Sec14.htm
Iraq Body Count
http://www.iraqbodycount.net/database
Iraq Coalition Casualties
http://icasualties.org/oif/
Jewish immigrants in Palestine
R Khamaisi, The distribution of Jewish immigrants in Palestine before and after the establishment of the State of Israel, 2002: http://geo.haifa.ac.il/~khamaisi/papers/jews_immeg.doc

Ministry of Defence (UK)
Defence analytical services: http://www.dasa.mod.uk/
Reports for researchers:
http://www.mod.uk/DefenceInternet/AboutDefence/
CorporatePublications/Reports/ReportsForResearchers/

Oil and Gas Directory
An industrial research on oil & gas sectors of Middle East
countries: http://www.oilandgasdirectory.com/ogd/res_
prof/middle_east.pdf

OnWar.com
North Yemeni civil war 1962-1970, armed conflict
events data: http://www.onwar.com/aced/data/yankee/
yemennorthciv1962.htm
Algerian War of independence 1954-1962, armed conflict
events data: http://www.onwar.com/aced/data/alpha/
falgeria1954.htm

Population in Egypt
Social Research Centre: http://www.aucegypt.
edu/src/wsite1/background/nationalprofile/
Population%20in%20Egypt.htm

Qadhafi's personal website
http://www.algathafi.org/index-en.htm

Saudi-US Relations Information Service
http://www.saudi-us-relations.org

Sykes-Picot Agreement
http://www.firstworldwar.com/source/sykespicot.htm

UN Development Programme
Annual Human Development Reports: http://hdr.undp.
org/reports
Egypt Human Development Report, 2004: http://www.
undp.org.eg/publications/HDP-2004-E%20.pdf

UN Information System on the Question of Palestine
Report of the Palestine Royal Commission, presented
July 1937: http://domino.un.org/unispal.nsf/0/
08e38a718201458b052565700072b358?OpenDocument

UN Relief and Works Agency
Palestinian refugee camp profiles: http://www.un.org/
unrwa/refugees/camp-profiles.html

UN Security Council
UN Security Council resolutions: http://www.un.org/
documents/scres.htm

US Committee on Refugees and Immigrants
World refugee survey, 2005: http://www.refugees.org/
worldmap.aspx

US Department of Energy
Global energy sanctions: http://www.eia.doe.gov/emeu/
cabs/sanction.html
Libya country analysis brief: http://www.eia.doe.gov/
emeu/cabs/libya.html
Non-OPEC fact sheet: http://www.eia.doe.gov/emeu/cabs/
nonopec.html
OPEC brief: http://www.eia.doe.gov/emeu/cabs/opec.html
Persian Gulf oil and gas exports fact sheet: http://www.
eia.doe.gov/emeu/cabs/pgulf.html
World oil market and oil price chronologies, 1970-2004:
http://www.eia.doe.gov/emeu/cabs/chron.html
World oil transit chokepoints: http://www.eia.doe.gov/
emeu/cabs/choke.html

US Department of the Treasury
Office of Foreign Asset Control, What you need to know
about US economic sanctions, Iran:
http://www.webiran.com/ofacguide.pdf
Office of Foreign Asset Control, Sanction programme
summaries, Libya: http://www.treas.gov/offices/
enforcement/ofac/programs/libya/libya.shtml
Office of Foreign Asset Control, Sanction programme
summaries, Syria: http://www.treas.gov/offices/
enforcement/ofac/programs/syria/syria.shtml

US Library of Congress
Country Studies/ Area Handbook Series: http://
countrystudies.us

US State Department
Background Notes: http://www.state.gov/r/pa/ei/bgn

Wikipedia
http://en.wikipedia.org/wiki/Main_Page

World Bank
Development Data and Statistics: http://www.worldbank.
org/data/countrydata

PHOTO CREDITS

INDEX